MW01596732

CLUTTER

*Replacing Chaos, Confusion, and Captivity in Your
Life with Peace, Purpose, and Freedom!*

PATRICK CANNON

WESTBOW°
PRESS
A DIVISION OF THOMAS NELSON
& ZONDERVAN

WestBow Press books may be ordered through booksellers or by contacting:

WestBow Press
A Division of Thomas Nelson & Zondervan
1663 Liberty Drive
Bloomington, IN 47403
www.westbowpress.com
1 (866) 928-1240

ISBN: 978-1-4908-4327-8 (sc)
ISBN: 978-1-4908-4328-5 (e)

Library of Congress Control Number: 2014911977

Printed in the United States of America.

WestBow Press rev. date: 7/16/2014

Contents

Dedication vii

Preface ix

Acknowledgement xiii

3 Dreams xv

Chapter 1   Clutter Defined 1

Chapter 2   My Past.. 17

Chapter 3   Worry 31

Chapter 4   Unforgiveness... 47

Chapter 5   Fear 62

Chapter 6   Anger... 78

Chapter 7   Lust 90

Chapter 8   Keep Going!... 104

Dedication

This book is dedicated to all those who helped make it possible. My friends at That Neighborhood Church and those that volunteer on a regular basis. Especially my wife Kelly who put up with my whining throughout the process.

Finally this book is dedicated to my mom. She struggled until the day God took her home. Knowing someone's journey makes all the difference in the world.

Preface

If someone would have told me five years ago that I would be writing a book based on 3 dreams I had on the same night, I would have told them they were smoking crack! This will be my 30th year in ministry. Through most of that time I've been ministering to children and their families. I have spent countless hours counseling families, moms and dads who's lives look great on the outside but are deteriorating on the inside. At one time I was on staff at one of the fastest growing churches in the country. For almost 10 years it was non-stop growth. From starting with 12 kids on a weekend to over 1200, it was a children's pastor's dream. My ministry was successful to say the least. But in the midst of running at break neck speed something toxic was taking place on the inside of me. I continued this pace even after I left the ministry to help build into my oldest son. I went right into planning an animation studio. The cycle continued as I put in countless hours trying to build my business while volunteering at another church. Needless to say my business never really took off. I ended up working at a print shop I used to own. Talk about humbling.

Fast forward to 2007 when I accepted a staff position at another mega church. I had gone through some pretty tough circumstances, but this seemed like a chance to move forward. Even though I tried to pace myself into the new position, I found myself getting into the same old rut.

At the end of 2009 God called me out of a very comfortable ministry situation into one of the most dangerous impoverished areas in Toledo, Ohio. Planting a church is hard enough, let alone trying to plant one in the hood. Lots of poverty, lots of drugs and an overwhelming amount of oppression. It was in this environment that God began to get my attention. I had spent my whole Christian life running forward. I wanted my life to count. Maybe the only way God knew to get my attention was while I sleeping. Whatever the reason, it was during one night that everything began to change. I had collected some very toxic clutter in my life that was causing me chaos, confusion and captivity. Whether I had ignored it, excused it or was just plain ignorant of it, God knew it was time for me to do some soul searching. Over the next months as I was in counseling I discover just how deep this clutter had collected. Some of it had affected me for over 40 years! As I began to work on identifying it and began the cleaning process I noticed a difference in how I dealt with life. I was gaining new freedom, peace and purpose in my life.

Then I had the courage to develop a series that I preached in our church as well as others titled "Clutter". It was during this time that I saw how many others were being held hostage by things like their past, worry and fear. Desperately wanting to experience the freedom God talks about. I was encouraged to write this book over and over again. What you are about to read is the result of not only my journey but also many others who I have counseled over the years.

My prayer is that as you read my story and others, God would encourage you to come face to face with those areas that have held you hostage for years and have the courage to start the cleaning process.

Acknowledgement

Special thanks to the Lana, Paul and Christopher Shryock. Without your help this would still be sitting in a drawer somewhere gathering dust!

3 Dreams

Nothing really spectacular happened that day. As the pastor of a church in one of the most impoverished areas in the country, my days are usually filled with meeting the needs of our neighbors while trying to point them towards Jesus. It's a rewarding, depressing, energizing, eye opening, confusing and faith stretching job all at the same time! At the end of the day when my head hits the pillow, I'm out in a matter of seconds. I usually sleep through the night, except for the typical "call of nature" in the middle of the night. Yeah, I'm getting older.

I'm one of those weird people that remember their dreams and could even tell you some of the dreams I had as a child. There was the time when I was visiting my grandma in Colorado. Where I dreamed that a large horned creature slowly opened the door, ran into my room and jumped on my bed. (I swear I felt my bed move as I woke up full of fear.) There were also Superboy dreams I used to have. I saved an elementary school from a tornado, stopped a flood from destroying our town and rescued my wife and I from some weird cult-like church by throwing cars in the parking lot. As a side note; my Superboy dreams stopped after I spent some time talking to a counselor to work through some kind of "rescue everyone" thing I had going on. Since then I haven't had any more Superboy dreams. Go figure.

Back to Tuesday night. It wasn't that I had a really weird dream. It was the fact that I had three dreams in a row that were all different but, had the same message. I want to say right off the bat that I haven't had any authentic Pentecostal experiences. Although I did work at a charismatic church for a while and tried really hard to get the whole "speaking in tongues" thing down, but it just didn't take for me. I guess I'm not very spiritual or something. On the other hand, I'm not saying supernatural things don't happen. I've experienced plenty of "God realities" while pastoring our little church in the hood. What I'm saying is, I wasn't searching for God's anointing, direction or confirmation about anything that night.

Dream #1
I was working at a print shop that I used to manage back in the early 1990's. I was working on one of the presses when my boss approached me. He was about to go on a trip and wanted to leave me in charge. The only problem was that he was waiting for me to clean up the clutter that had collected around my area before he left. My boss just stood there, staring at me. I finally asked him if he was leaving soon. He said he was waiting for me to clean up the clutter. As soon as I did he would

leave me in charge. I woke up, went to the bathroom. Nature was calling! I climbed back in bed and quickly fell back asleep.

Dream #2

I was a little kid again. I was in my room getting ready to go out and play. My mom came in my room and looked at the mess that surrounded me. I asked her, "Mommy, can I go out and play?" She didn't seem to hear me because she was focused on the mess in my room. So I asked her again, "Mommy, can I go out and play with my friends now?" Then she looked at me and said, "Oh, honey, remember I asked you to clean up your room before you could go outside? I'm so sorry but you'll have to clean up your room before you can go outside and play with your friends". She wasn't mean about it, but stated it in a matter of fact manner.

I woke up again and thought to myself, that was weird. I tossed and turned for about an hour and then fell back to sleep.

Dream #3

In my third dream I was standing in a large room. The room was filled with fog. For some reason I knew I needed to get to the other side but every time I would take a few steps I would trip over something. After about ten steps my frustration level began to rise. There was junk all over the floor that I had to step around or over. Finally the fog started to lift. As it became easier to see I discovered the whole room was filled with all kinds of junk! Everything from candy wrappers to car parts. Every step was hindered by junk that was in my way. Out of frustration I yelled, "WOULD SOMEBODY CLEAN UP THIS MESS!?"

I woke up and sat up in bed staring into space. My heart was racing. I had gotten the message loud and clear! It's time to clean up the clutter in your life, Pat.

Chapter One

Clutter Defined

"If a cluttered desk is a sign of a cluttered mind, of what, then, is an empty desk a sign?" Albert Einstein.

If one's going to title a book "Clutter", it's a good idea to define the word. Webster defines Clutter as a "disorderly heap". If you have every watched the TV show "Hoarders" it is something you gradually accumulate until the negative effect on your life becomes overwhelming.

Believe it or not, clutter is a Biblical concept. In chapter 11 of Hebrews, the apostle Paul describes what faith is, why we need it, and why God loves it. This is followed by example after example of individuals who lived their lives by faith in the midst of unpredictable circumstances. Every one of them, not knowing the outcome, decided to trust in God's directional promises.

At the end of chapter 11, Paul said every one of them received God's approval because of their faith, and they are waiting for us to finish the race so they could receive what was promised. No pressure there! Chapter 12 starts off with the word, "Therefore". In other words, because of what you just read, this is what you should do.

Hebrews 12:1 (NLT)
1 Therefore, since we are surrounded by such a huge crowd of witnesses to the life of faith,

The "crowd" Paul is talking about includes everyone he had just spoken about in Chapter 11 through those living today. All chose to follow God's lead. All without knowing the outcome, trusting in His promises. All witnessed God's faithfulness.

Paul wants to let us know about a life changing truth. It's the number one thing that cannot only destroy our faith; but keep us from witnessing God's power and experiencing His blessing, protection and direction in our lives. It can actually prevent us from experiencing what I call "God realities". What's a God reality? I don't know about you but I'm like many Jesus followers who have gone to church and read the Bible. I have both *read* and *heard* about God. A God reality is when we actually get to see and experience something that can only be described as supernatural.

For example, when I was eight my family lived on the outskirts of Omaha, Nebraska. The highway department was starting a major project that would bring a highway right by our little rural neighborhood. It was winter and a major snowstorm had just dumped nearly 15 inches of snow. My mom and I were driving back from the store. The roads weren't terrible, but they were snow covered and slick. Our last approach was a long steep hill led to a curve, and end with one more turn into our neighborhood. About half way down the hill our full sized station wagon began to slide. My mom's approach was classic. She took her hands off the wheel and screamed. As we picked up speed, I remembered the steep drop off on the other side of the curve. Our speed increased and all my little eight year old brain could do was to ask God to not let us die! Everything happened extremely fast. As we approached the curve, I saw the big pile of snow in front of us. In a matter of seconds we hit the snow and our car came to a sudden stop just inches from going over the edge. My mom and I looked at each other and cried. We had just experienced a God reality. This was evidenced when the wrecker came to pull us out and the driver told us how "lucky" we were because just moments before the plow had come by and pushed all the snow against the curve. In the midst of our fear and uncertainty we experienced God's protection in our lives.

Clutter can prevent us from experiencing God realities in our lives. They hold us back from diving into a place where God becomes real.

In the rest of Hebrews 12:1, Paul explains more about clutter.

Hebrews 12:1 (NLT)
1 Therefore, since we are surrounded by such a huge crowd of witnesses to the life of faith, let us strip off every weight that slows us down, especially the sin that so easily trips us up. And let us run with endurance the race God has set before us.

Paul describes two kinds of clutter that can prevent us from not just winning the race called life; but finishing it in a strong manner.

Clutter Number One
"Every weight that slows us down".
It's important to notice that Paul isn't necessarily saying that "every weight" is a sin. Clutter is something that constantly gets in our way. It could be an unhealthy relationship, a bad habit, or even our past.

Clutter Number Two
"Especially the sin that so easily trips us up."
These are the sins that we go back to over and over again. Not only is it a sin we go back to but it's a sin that constantly trips us up. For many of you reading this, it's a no brainer to figure out what that sin is. And it's different for every one of us. Let's be honest we know which sins in our lives cause us to stumble and fall over and over again.

HOW BAD IS IT?
As I began to think about the impact of clutter in my life and the lives those I have counseled over the

years, I discovered clutter can have three toxic effects in our lives.

CLUTTER CAUSES CONFUSION

In my town of Toledo, Ohio there are four bridges a driver can use to cross the Maumee River, a major waterway that leads into Lake Erie. The newest and largest bridge is the Veteran's Glass City Skyway. Standing at 400 ft. high, with a length of 2.5 miles, this is by far my favorite bridge to cross. I love coming up over the top to see the sky line and the river below. I remember one foggy day as I was crossing the bridge; my vision was limited to what was directly in front of me. Everything below the bridge was covered by thick fog. Anything I normally would see on a clear day was hidden. No skyline, no river, just fog. If I didn't know the area I would have easy to gotten confused and missed my exit.

When we have clutter in our lives it creates a sense of confusion. It creates a foggy perspective on what's ahead. It takes something that is normally easy to see, familiar and easy to navigate and makes it unfamiliar, cloudy and hard to navigate.

CLUTTER CAUSES CHAOS

Are there any "messes" in the house?! I tend to be a "messy". I've tried my best to improve in this are over the years but it's an unending battle. My wife puts up with a lot! To give you an example, when we were first married we bought our first house, a mobile home. It was a 14 foot by 80 foot rectangle with three bedrooms, a living room, kitchen and two bathrooms. At that time in my life I was really into building crazy things. For some reason I got it into my brain that I wanted to build a folding boat. I didn't even know if there ever was such a thing. This was before the internet, so I went to the library and found a book from the early 1900s with plans for, you guessed it, a folding boat. On the outside looking in it seemed fairly simple, straight forward and inexpensive. The only problem was there was no place to build it. The only place I could think of was our living room. So with lots of convincing, my wonderful wife gave me the green light as long as I "cleaned up" after each building session. The first week went pretty well. But after that I would "forget" to put away a couple tools, which my amazing wife would trip over. Then there were those times I would "sort of" vacuum the carpet and miss a couple nails or screws. The clutter began to accumulate until it even got to me! Every time I walked into the house I would feel my stress level increase. I could just imagine what my wife was feeling! Eventually my life began to "feel" like my mess. I felt like I couldn't think straight or concentrate until I cleaned up the mess.

Needless to say, I never finished my folding boat. It became a boat bed for my oldest son. I had great intensions but my clutter created so much chaos it prevented me from reaching my goal. That's what clutter does. Even its presence can cause our stress levels to rise. We can lose focus on what's important. Everything can seem to close in around us.

CLUTTER CREATES CAPTIVITY
The worst thing about clutter is it creates captivity in our lives. We can actually let it hold us hostage. It keeps us from moving forward with our lives. One of Satan's goals in the life of a believer is to hold them captive in their own clutter. He knows if he can hold you captive, you are less effective at building God's kingdom and reaching your potential in Christ.

Our neighborhood is filled with individuals and families who are being held hostage in generational poverty. Generational poverty is defined by those that have grown up in poverty for at least two generations. This has had a devastating impact on our community. It has created an oppressive culture. When you are in generational poverty you begin to tell yourself that you do not have options. Worse, is the fact that you don't know you have options!

Clutter, if left to continue, can create similarly oppressive chains as those in generational poverty.

THE BIG LIE
The scariest thing about clutter is we can actually convince ourselves that because we go to church, know "churchy" stuff, say "churchy" things and are involved in "churchy" activities, God looks past our clutter. I've thought this in my own life. Hey, I'm a pastor. I'm

doing all these wonderful things for God. I'm leading people to Jesus, feeding the hungry, clothing the naked and ministering to widows and orphans. I'm doing all the "right stuff" so God will bless me even though I have clutter in my life that I haven't addressed or I have ignored. The crazy thing is I had convinced myself that I could actually manipulate God by doing the right things on the outside while my inside is filled with "the weight that slows me down" or worse "the sin that so easily trips me up".

My self-deception was unmasked when I came to a passage of scripture found in the book of Jeremiah. If there is one job I would never ever want to have, it was Jeremiah's! This young man was called by God as a prophet. His job was to tell the nation of Israel that God was done messing around. God's people had let so much clutter into their lives that they were actually worshipping other gods and even sacrificing their own children! Jeremiah's job was to warn them that if they didn't clean up their clutter, God's blessing and protection would be taken away. (Oh, and as a side note, God also told Jeremiah they would hate him and his message.) Now that's a great job description! Jeremiah was betrayed by his own family and friends. His hometown turned their backs on him. He was beaten and whipped numerous times. He was thrown down a well to rot. He was put in prison. And he battled depression. Jeremiah wept over the sins and clutter of God's people so much that he is known as the weeping prophet.

God didn't beat around the bush when it came to his "kids". Israel was supposed to know God and follow Him. They were God followers. And just like today, those calling themselves Jesus followers had a regular pattern of "going to church" every week. They had this crazy idea that their relationship with God centered on how they acted and were perceived at church. Somehow the "act" of going to church validated to everyone that God was pleased with them, was blessing and protecting them, and because they went to church all was well. Sound familiar?

God has a great way of pushing away our own self-deception and exposing the truth of how we are really living our lives.

Check out how God views the clutter in our life and how we think the "act" of going to church somehow makes it all better.

Jeremiah 7:1-11 (NLT)
1 The Lord gave another message to Jeremiah. He said.
2 "Go to the entrance of the Lord's Temple, and give this message to the people: 'O Judah, listen to this message from the Lord! Listen to it, all of you who worship here!
3 This is what the Lord of Heaven's Armies, the God of Israel, says: "'Even now, if you quit your evil ways, I will let you stay in your own land.

4 But don't be fooled by those who promise you safety simply because the Lord's Temple is here. They chant, "The Lord's Temple is here! The Lord's Temple is here!"

5 But I will be merciful only if you stop your evil thoughts and deeds and start treating each other with justice;

6 only if you stop exploiting foreigners, orphans, and widows; only if you stop your murdering; and only if you stop harming yourselves by worshiping idols.

7 Then I will let you stay in this land that I gave to your ancestors to keep forever.

8 "'Don't be fooled into thinking that you will never suffer because the Temple is here. It's a lie!

9 Do you really think you can steal, murder, commit adultery, lie, and burn incense to Baal and all those other new gods of yours,

10 and then come here and stand before me in my Temple and chant, "We are safe!"—only to go right back to all those evils again?

11 Don't you yourselves admit that this Temple, which bears my name, has become a den of thieves? Surely I see all the evil going on there. I, the Lord, have spoken!

In case you used the latest speed reading techniques to get through those verses, check out how The Message transliteration puts it.

Jeremiah 7:1-11 (MSG)

1 The Message from God to Jeremiah:

2 "Stand in the gate of God's Temple and preach this Message. "Say, 'Listen, all you people of Judah who come through these gates to worship God

3 God-of-the-Angel-Armies, Israel's God, has this to say to you: "'Clean up your act—the way you live, the things you do—so I can make my home with you in this place.

4 Don't for a minute believe the lies being spoken here—"This is God's Temple, God's Temple, God's Temple!"

5 Total nonsense! Only if you clean up your act (the way you live, the things you do), only if you do a total spring cleaning on the way you live and treat your neighbors,

6 only if you quit exploiting the street people and orphans and widows, no longer taking advantage of innocent people on this very site and no longer destroying your souls by using this Temple as a front for other gods—

7 only then will I move into your neighborhood. Only then will this country I gave your ancestors be my permanent home, my Temple.

8 "'Get smart! Your leaders are handing you a pack of lies, and you're swallowing them!

9 Use your heads! Do you think you can rob and murder, have sex with the neighborhood wives, tell lies nonstop, worship the local gods, and buy every novel religious commodity on the market

10 —and then march into this Temple, set apart for my worship, and say, "We're safe!" thinking that the place itself gives you a license to go on with all this outrageous sacrilege?

11 A cave full of criminals! Do you think you can turn this Temple, set apart for my worship, into something like that? Well, think again. I've got eyes in my head. I can see what's going on.'" God's Decree!

I NEED A DOCTOR OR AT LEAST A DOCTOR'S OFFICE!

What Jeremiah is describing is what happened to me about a month ago. I have a lower back that just loves to rebel and go places that no lower back should ever go! I was at a meeting at the local coffee shop when I dropped something under my table, so I decided to pick it. Little did I know that was all it was going to take for the "rebel" to rebel. I knew the minute I stood up that I was in trouble. By the time my meeting was over I could barely make it to my truck. I looked pretty pathetic. For about three days I laid on my back waiting for the rebellion to end. I finally decided to make an appointment with my doctor. (Guys are slow like that.) The day came for the appointment. I walked into the waiting room, signed the little sheet and then waited for over 30 minutes, while thumbing through the latest golf magazine. (I don't even golf!) They called my name and took me to the back. I took a seat on the paper covered table and waited another 20 minutes. Finally the doctor came in and asked, "So Mr. Cannon what can I do for you?" I replied, "Hey doc, thanks for seeing me! See you next time". I just got up and left! I left fully expecting to get better just because I walked into the doctor's office and went through the motions. The only problem is, I never let the doctor examine me. I never let him figure out the source of pain but I expected a full recovery.

Ok, so I didn't just walk out, but for so many of us who claim to be Christ's followers, that's exactly what we do. We go through the motions of church attendance expecting God to continue blessing, protecting and providing for us, while our lives are filled with clutter. Oh, you might be saved from the fires of hell, but your life here on earth will continue to be filled with confusion, chaos and captivity until you start cleaning out the clutter.

In the rest of the book I'm going to share with you six different kinds of clutter that I have encountered the most in other people's lives as well as my own. Each chapter will start off introducing you to a particular kind of clutter, how it affects us and what steps you can take to start cleaning it out of your life.

Before I end this chapter I want to give you five actions steps that will get you ready to not only face your clutter, but prepare you to clean it out for good.

Step One

Realize we all have clutter. You are not alone. I'm always amazed when someone shares with me the clutter they struggle with as if they are the only one. Even the apostle Paul admitted in Romans Chapter 7 that he had clutter in his life.

Romans 7:15-17 (NLT)
15 I don't really understand myself, for I want to do what is right, but I don't do it. Instead, I do what I hate.
16 But if I know that what I am doing is wrong, this shows that I agree that the law is good.
17 So I am not the one doing wrong; it is sin living in me that does it.

Paul admits it's the clutter in his life that is causing the problem. The first place to start is to admit clutter exists.

Step Two

Write out the clutter you keep tripping over. Get out a sheet of paper and actually write out the "weights" that are slowing you down, the sin that keeps tripping you up, the clutter in your life. Be extremely honest; don't hide anything. When I sat down to do this it wasn't pretty. Here are a few questions that might help.

What habit is currently holding you hostage? Remember, this might not be a sin, but you go back to it over and over again. It effects how you view yourself and keeps you from moving forward in your life, your relationship with others and with God.

What sin do you keep tripping over? You know it's there. You've asked for forgiveness more times than you care to count. You can't seem to stop tripping over the same sin. In the deepest recesses of your heart you want to be free, but it's holding you hostage creating confusion and captivity.

The number one thing in my life that is holding me back is.

Step Three

Tell God about your clutter. Let's face it, He already knows it's there. He's been patiently waiting for you to admit it. I recommend saying it out loud. Once you do, you allow God's Spirit to start doing the work He's been waiting to do. He was just waiting for permission. God's a perfect gentleman. He won't start the work until you ask Him to!

Step Four

Find a trusted friend to hold you accountable. If you have an addictive personality like me, you will need someone to help you stay on course. I have numerous men who keep me accountable in various areas of my life. It's healthy and it's Biblical.

Step Five

Ask for God's help. Since God has been waiting for permission to start cleaning out your clutter, once you say yes, He is ready and willing to do the work required to set you free! Your job is to believe He will give you the strength to do whatever it takes.

Are you ready to start cleaning out that clutter? When you start the cleaning process and the fog starts to lift, you will be amazed at the freedom you will feel. When the weight starts to lift, your ability to run this race called life will increase, and it will feel less confusing and more focused. Don't go another day filled with clutter. Start now! Open up the closet of your life and start cleaning!

Chapter 2

My Past

"The past can't hurt you any more, not unless you let it" Alan Moore

Let me share five brief descriptions with you about the backgrounds of five famous individuals.

1) He was born in Detroit. His mother couldn't read and only had a 3rd grade education. She married at 13 and divorced 10 years later leaving them in extreme poverty. He was a poor student with a huge chip on his shoulder that lead to violent angry outbursts. He was known to attack his classmates at the slightest provocation. He ended up at the bottom of his class.

2) Many of his teachers told him he was too stupid to learn. He was fired from numerous jobs because they said he was too unproductive. He had over 1,000 failures before he was met with success.

3) In his first attempts he froze on stage he was jeered at and booed off stage as a failure.

4) She suffered verbal and physical abuse growing up and was treated unfairly and fired from her television reporter job because she was considered unfit for television.

5) He missed almost 9,000 shots in his career and lost over 300 games. He was cut from his high school team because of his lack of ability.

In order of their stories...

Ben Carson - Number one pediatric neurosurgeon in the world.

Thomas Edison - Invented the practical light bulb and over 1,000 other inventions.

Jerry Seinfeld - Actor comedian

Oprah Winfrey - Talk show host

Michael Jordan - Basketball star

Oh, and there's one more story I need to share.

He was born into a dysfunctional broken family. He was physically and mentally abused by his own mother for years. He was sexually abused by a neighbor. He grew up thinking he was somehow defective. He spent years dragging his past with him where he went. He tried to block out the pain of his past through addictions. From the outside he was viewed as someone who had their life together, but on the inside he was being held hostage by his past. He spent years counseling others how to not let their past define their futures while dragging his own around with him.

If you haven't guessed it yet, the last one is me. It's amazing to me how we can live our lives helping others by speaking truth into them while not letting it impact our own. I wonder if you were to describe your past in just a few sentences what you would say. I wonder not only how you would describe it, but how you are letting it define your life today and your future. Before we get too far into this chapter, I want to remind you of something that will encourage you; it's an old saying, but very true.

"Every saint has a past, every sinner has a future".

No matter who you are, you have a past. The important thing isn't that you have a past, it's whether your past is causing confusion, chaos and captivity in your life. The truth about our past is very important.

Truth #1 - *I cannot change it!*
Remember the movie "Back to the Future"? Marty McFly and his professor friend Dr. Emmet Brown built a car that could travel back in time. Let me tell you, there are many things I wish I could go back and change the past. But the reality is we can't go back and we can't change what we did in the past. We can only change what we are doing right now.

Truth #2 - *My Past is History*
I love to watch documentaries, especially the ones that talk about past history. The best documentaries stick to the facts and don't sugar coat them. They tell

the story as it really happened. They usually interview people who were there or quote from diaries. They're not trying to change history; they are trying to tell history. It's the same with our past. It's been written in stone. Regardless of how we feel about it, it stands as history. We can either let our history define our future or leave it for what it is; past history.

Truth #3 - *When I hold on to my past, I give other people and experiences permission to hold me hostage.*

This is probably one of the most common issues I have faced in other people's lives as well as in my own life. Holding onto the clutter of your past can actually tie you up and manipulate you like a puppet on a string.

No matter what kind of past you have, I want you to know that you're in good company! In fact, God loves embracing, empowering and releasing those who are being held hostage by their past. The Bible is full of men and women with dysfunctional, broken lives when God gets hold of them. He doesn't look at their past. He doesn't look at who they were or what they did. He only looks at who He knows they can become.

Probably one of my favorite stories centers around an individual that had every right to let his past define his future. Let's face it, sometimes we view some of these Bible characters as some kind of super spiritual giants of the church. We look at what they have become and forget what and who they were. The next time you read one of their stories don't focus on who they are now, focus on who they were and how they let Jesus define their future.

Peter's Past

Peter's first real encounter with Jesus takes place in the midst of a normal work day. For a fisherman on the sea of Galilee, your "day" actually lasts all night. For Peter it wasn't one of those days to write home about; especially when your catch determined your paycheck. After a night of absolute failure, the sun comes up, the nets are brought in and everyone quietly murmurs as they paddle back to shore. Once there, it's time to wash out the nets, picking out the seaweed and the other muck left behind. It's was during this moment that Jesus walks up and asks Peter if he would mind going back out. I know what would have going through my mind! Peter gives in and Jesus climbs in his boat. If I were Peter I would have been wondering' "what does Jesus want with my boat?" I've never seen him fish before!

Jesus has Peter stop the boat so he can preach His morning sermon to the crowd. After He finished, Jesus asks Peter to do something that probably took him by surprise. Jesus told him, a professional fisherman, where to catch fish! Peter took the net, threw it over board and began to draw it back in. In a matter of minutes it was overflowing with fish. So many fish that he yelled to the rest of the fisherman to get their boats out there to help. Everybody was excited and panicking at the same time! They filled their boats until they overflowed.

I'm sure there was laughter, shouting maybe a little happy cussing. After the last fish was pulled in, everyone looked at each other in quiet hushed tones. That's when Peter realized what he had just experienced. That's when the reality of who Jesus was sunk in.

Luke 5:8-11 (NLT)
8 When Simon Peter realized what had happened; he fell to his knees before Jesus and said, "Oh, Lord, please leave me—I'm too much of a sinner to be around you."

Stop right there! Sometimes when we read these stories we move too fast! Peter is saying to Jesus, "Get away from me! You don't know my past. And if you did you wouldn't want to be around me." Peter is saying to himself, "Because of my past I don't deserve your love." At the very beginning Peter is struggling with his past. He is already telling himself a new life is out of his reach because of his past. Once Peter encountered Jesus and saw Him for who He was, his past flooded his heart and his response is like ours when we come to God or connect with other people.

If you knew my past you wouldn't love and except me!

Listen to how Jesus responds.

9 For he was awestruck by the number of fish they had caught, as were the others with him.
10 His partners, James and John, the sons of Zebedee, were also amazed. Jesus replied to Simon, "Don't be afraid! From now on you'll be fishing for people!"
11 And as soon as they landed, they left everything and followed Jesus.

Jesus' response has nothing to do with Peter's past but has everything to do with Peter's future! Imagine what that did to Peter. He was expecting a rejection. He was expecting a rebuke. Instead he received grace!

The next encounter that Peter had could have scarred him for life. Peter lived with Jesus for three years. He watched Him perform miracle after miracle. He pledged his life to Jesus and basically told him he would die for Him if needed. Peter was all in! Until, Jesus got arrested.

Peter followed from a safe distance while they dragged Jesus to the front court yard of the high priest's (Caiaphas) house. Peter tried not to be noticed,as he mixed in with the crowd. Grunts, groans, curses, laughter, jokes and accusations filled the air. Peter watched Jesus being abused by the drunk guards. He sat with the guards hoping they wouldn't notice who he was.

The first one to come up to him was a little servant girl. She stopped and looked at Peter. "Hey I remember you. I saw you with Jesus!" Everyone, and I mean everyone turned and looked at Peter. His response was immediate and accompanied by a little chuckle. "I don't know what you're talking about." Peter got up and walked over by the gate to the court yard hoping to hide himself. Another servant girl came up and moved around to get a better look at Peter. "Yeah, this guy was with Jesus, I know it!," she said. Again all eyes on Peter. "I don't even know this guy Jesus!" Peter knew his plan to conceal himself wasn't working. But, time passed and he moved to another part of the courtyard. He had almost convinced himself his plan worked when a small group came up and stared at him for a few moments. Then one of them said, "We know your one them. Your accent gives you away!" Peter had enough! This time he spoke so loud that everyone heard him. "If I'm lying may God strike me dead! I DON'T KNOW JESUS!"

It was at that time that Peter stole a look at Jesus. The rooster crowed just like Jesus said it would. Peter was broken. He left, sobbing as he went. Peter, the one who lived with Jesus three years, the one who saw miracle after miracle, lived with God in human form, chose to go the other way.

Think about the worst regret you have in your past. The one event, conversation or experience that gnaws at you every time you look in the mirror. The one thing you would love to do over. That's Peter.

The amazing thing about God is that He doesn't leave us captive to our past. He desperately wants to release us from our past in order to start building a new future. How this takes place in Peter's life is how God wants to help release you and I from our past and start moving to a new future. Peter is dealing with his denial of Jesus, the death of Jesus and the resurrection of Jesus. Talk about needing some "R and R"! Peter decides to go back to the only thing he knows. Read what happens next in John 21:3-22

John 21:3-23 (NLT)

3 Simon Peter said, "I'm going fishing." "We'll come, too," they all said. So they went out in the boat, but they caught nothing all night.
4 At dawn Jesus was standing on the beach, but the disciples couldn't see who he was.
5 He called out, "Fellows, have you caught any fish?" "No," they replied.
6 Then he said, "Throw out your net on the right-hand side of the boat, and you'll get some!" So they did, and they couldn't haul in the net because there were so many fish in it.
7 Then the disciple Jesus loved said to Peter, "It's the Lord!" When Simon Peter heard that it was the Lord, he put on his tunic (for he had stripped for work), jumped into the water, and headed to shore.
8 The others stayed with the boat and pulled the loaded net to the shore, for they were only about a hundred yards from shore.

9 When they got there, they found breakfast waiting for them—fish cooking over a charcoal fire, and some bread.

10 "Bring some of the fish you've just caught," Jesus said.

11 So Simon Peter went aboard and dragged the net to the shore. There were 153 large fish, and yet the net hadn't torn.

12 "Now come and have some breakfast!" Jesus said. None of the disciples dared to ask him, "Who are you?" They knew it was the Lord.

13 Then Jesus served them the bread and the fish.

14 This was the third time Jesus had appeared to his disciples since he had been raised from the dead.

15 After breakfast Jesus asked Simon Peter, "Simon son of John, do you love me more than these?" "Yes, Lord," Peter replied, "you know I love you." "Then feed my lambs," Jesus told him.

16 Jesus repeated the question: "Simon son of John, do you love me?" "Yes, Lord," Peter said, "you know I love you." "Then take care of my sheep," Jesus said.

17 A third time he asked him, "Simon son of John, do you love me?" Peter was hurt that Jesus asked the question a third time. He said, "Lord, you know everything. You know that I love you." Jesus said, "Then feed my sheep.

Stop! Let me ask you a question. How many times did Jesus ask Peter the question, "Do you love me?"

Three. That wasn't an accident! When God comes to us He doesn't want to rehash our past. This was the first conversation Peter had with Jesus since he denied Him. I'm sure that the only thing going through his mind as he swam towards shore was, "what I'm I going to say? What is Jesus going to say?" Maybe Peter was expecting a rebuke. But to Peter's surprise, not once did Jesus bring up his past. Jesus wasn't concerned about the past, He wants to know what Peter was going to do about his future.

Let's continue.

18 "I tell you the truth, when you were young, you were able to do as you liked; you dressed yourself and went wherever you wanted to go. But when you are old, you will stretch out your hands, and others will dress you and take you where you don't want to go."
19 Jesus said this to let him know by what kind of death he would glorify God. Then Jesus told him, "Follow me."
20 Peter turned around and saw behind them the disciple Jesus loved—the one who had leaned over to Jesus during supper and asked, "Lord, who will betray you?"
21 Peter asked Jesus, "What about him, Lord?"
22 Jesus replied, "If I want him to remain alive until I return, what is that to you? As for you, follow me."

Jesus is saying to Peter and He is saying to you and I, "When I think about you and your future I'm not counting your past against you. Your past doesn't have to define your future." Again, Jesus never mentioned Peter's past. Based on what we just read, here are three very important truths about your past.

My biggest sins are not too big for God's grace.

I am not what I have done. I am what God says I am.

I can't change my past, but Christ can change my future.

Let me bring this chapter to a close with an illustration of how this plays out.

Mirrors are crazy things. They never lie. They are the original WYSIWYG (What You See Is What You Get) screen. But, we are notorious in how we view ourselves when we look into a mirror, especially if you are letting your past define who you are. Below I have two different mirrors. One is what we tell ourselves based on our past. The other is what God says about us based on our future.

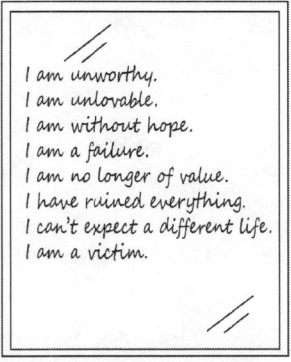

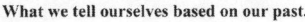

I am unworthy.
I am unlovable.
I am without hope.
I am a failure.
I am no longer of value.
I have ruined everything.
I can't expect a different life.
I am a victim.

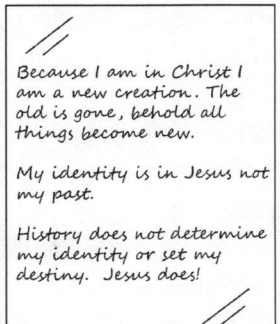

Because I am in Christ I am a new creation. The old is gone, behold all things become new.

My identity is in Jesus not my past.

History does not determine my identity or set my destiny. Jesus does!

What we tell ourselves based on our past. **What God says about us based on our future**

I have learned the best way to start cleaning out the clutter of my past is to begin with truth. Here is the truth about what God says about you!

2 Corinthians 5:17 (NLT)
17 This means that anyone who belongs to Christ has become a new person. The old life is gone; a new life has begun!

Ephesians 2:10 (NLT)
10 For we are God's masterpiece. He has created us anew in Christ Jesus, so we can do the good things he planned for us long ago.

Take some time today to let these truths sink in. You might not feel like a masterpiece, but remember God isn't looking at your past, He is looking at what you can become. I've included a list of verses for you to read and embrace. Every verse is a truth about God's view of you and your past. Ask God to put away the clutter of your past and replace it with the truth of your future with Him.

God's Views You As...

His Son or Daughter
He views you as a son or daughter. 2 Corinthians 6:17-18, 1 John 3:1, Romans 8:17
God chose to love you and make you His own! I Thessalonians 1:4

Valuable
Matthew 10:29-31
Luke 12:24

Forgiven
God promises to forgive our sins. I John 1:9
Once our sins are forgiven, God forgets them! Hebrews 10:17, Isaiah 43:25-26, Psalm 103:12
When we turn to God He wipes out our sin! Acts 3:19
God came up with a way to forgive you long before you were even born! I Peter 1:18-20
God's character is forgiveness! Psalm 86:4-5, 103:8-12
God's forgiveness brings us rest! Matthew 11:28-30
God lavishes His forgiveness on us! Ephesians 1:7-10
My forgiveness through Jesus can never be taken away! I Peter 1:3-4

Chapter 3

Worry

"Worry does not empty tomorrow of its sorrow. It empties today of its strength."
Corrie Ten Boom

Let me ask you a question. When is the last time you were really worried about something? Was it about your finances? Maybe it was an illness that was recently diagnosed. Whatever it was or is, worry can cause confusion, chaos and captivity in our lives. The crazy thing about worry is that it lays hidden underneath lots of other kinds of clutter. Worry can reveal, in front of God and others, the core of who we are. It reveals at our core how much we really trust God.

Over the last 2 years this had been very raw for me. I took just a few minutes to write out a few of the many things I was worried about:

1. Would our house sell?
2. Would our daughter Hannah be able to raise the rest of her money for Africa?

3. Would I be able to move my wife's sister from Florida to Alabama at get back in three days?
4. How are we going to raise $25,000 by the end of June?
5. Will we have enough in the offering to pay the bills this week?
6. Is this whole ministry going to blow up in my face?
7. How are we going to pay for a new furnace for the church?
8. Am I going to be able to renovate the parsonage in 20 days for us to move in?
9. How are we going to be able to sustain our key ministries that are growing?
10. How are we going to get the vocational center renovated?
11. Will I be able to raise my financial support next year?

Man, I better stop! I'm starting to get worried all over again! I could go on and on. I'm sure if you had time you could start coming up with a list as well. If we are honest, all of us have been worried about something at one time or another in our lives.

There are some basic truths about us or others we know when we become worriers. These truths manifest themselves in many different ways, but there are four that jump out.

#1 **When we worry, we live in the future, not the present.**

Below is a simple time line of someone's life. You will notice it's divided into 3 basics parts.

Past	Present	Future

As we talked about in the last chapter, our past is done. We can't do anything to change it. It is history. Your present is taking place as your read this. But the crazy thing is, every second that goes by becomes your past. Stop and think about that for a while over a cup of coffee! You can make decisions today that can actually affect your future. But, you can't know for certain what your future will bring. When we worry, it is almost always about what the future has in store. Worry has a very close cousin known as fear. And fear loves to hang out in the future. We'll tackle fear in Chapter 5.

#2 **When we worry we visualize the future in minute, gory detail.**

If you have kids, this happens quite often to you, especially if your kids are teenagers. We have four kids. All but one are grown and gone (for the moment, but you never know.) I have had sleepless nights over every one of them. Like, when my girls would be out with their friends and it started to get late. Then it got past late and beyond curfew. That's when I would start imagine all sorts of terrible things. Car accidents, abductions and emergency room calls. I would live it all in vivid color. Usually, I would be pacing back and forth while sweating my head off. That's when the phone would ring and almost put me into a coma! "Daddy? Sorry it's so late. I'm just going to stay at Robin's house, we're watching a movie." I would be so relieved they weren't dead in a ditch somewhere I would forget to scold them.

#3 When we worry we become false prophets.

Wouldn't it be terrible if everything we worried about came true? Talk about depressing, I wouldn't even want to get out of bed! Think about people in the Bible who were known as prophets. The reason they were known as prophets is because everything they said came true. If just ONE of their predictions didn't come to pass they were considered false prophets. In a now famous 1990 study, researchers Wells and Mathews at the University of Cincinnati discovered that 85% of what we worry about NEVER actually happens. The 15% of the time that something does happen, we handle it effectively 79% of the time. I'm no math whiz, but that would seem to mean that of all the things were worry about, only about 3% of the time something bad happens that we don't handle well.

It's like the story of an old woman who spent every day walking around her house carrying a bundle of twigs. She walked this same route every day for years, wearing a deep rut in the ground surrounding her home. One day a new neighbor stopped her and asked why she was doing this. She responded, "I'm keeping my home safe from tigers." The flabbergasted neighbor replied, "But this is Indiana! There are no tigers in Indiana!" The old woman replied, "See!"

#4 When we worry we don't want to listen to reason.

When you are in the thick of the "worry forest" you can't see the forest for the trees. No amount of convincing will tell you otherwise. About 16 years ago I had convinced myself that I had throat cancer. I'm a worry wart when it comes to my health anyway. I've watched way too many documentaries! Anyway, to say I was worried sick is an understatement. I went through a battery of tests, spent tons of money and the final diagnosis was that I wasn't drinking enough water. But, there was nothing you could say to me to convince me otherwise!

So let me ask you another question. Is worrying a sin or is it just one of those nutty things we do as human beings? What if worry revealed something deeper in us? Because at the core of our worry are some very, very intense dark conclusions we have made.

1. *There is no one who can really help me.*
2. *There is no one who can rescue me.*
3. *There is no one looking out for me.*

4. *I am alone in this world that operates by chance.*

I think God knows we are going to worry. In the Bible He asks us not to fear almost 350 times! He knows we are going to struggle with fear and worry.

Yosemite Half Dome

Worry Mountain

Have you ever tried to calm someone's worries? In 1982, I was on a short term mission trip in Lake Tahoe California. Yeah, I was "suffering" for Jesus. That's where I first met my wife, Kelly. One of the things we did was visit Yosemite National Park to climb Half Dome. This 10 plus mile hike takes about 12 hours to complete. You actually climb almost 5,000 feet. (It is so dangerous that you have to sign a release of liability form now before you attempt the climb. I get it, That way if you die, you won't sue them.) Most of the hike takes you past awesome rock formations, and, if it had recently rained, waterfalls. It was at the last 400 feet that I came face to face with "Worry Mountain".

A vertical perspective of the last 400 feet.

Anyway, the last 400 feet is almost 90 degrees straight up. The only thing you have to hold on to are two ropes and boards. If you slip off, you die. Kelly and I started our ascent. She was in front of me. At this point we were both dehydrated. I could tell Kelly wasn't doing well. It was about 98 degrees. We started climbing up the cables and Kelly stopped and said. "I'm afraid I can't make it." Oh, by the way, Kelly is a fainter. We have about 20 people behind us and once you start there is no turning back. We had about 300 feet to go, straight up. I confidently told her not to worry, that we we're almost there. Thirty feet later she said it again. "I don't think I can make it, I think I need to go back down." I told her again that we were almost there and that I was right behind her. She must have said that 10 times on the way up. Little did she know that we were a lot farther from the top than I led her to believe. In the back of my mind I'm going, "please don't faint!"

The thing I want you to understand is that it wasn't my words, "don't worry", that helped Kelly make it. It was who she turned to when she worried. When she felt like she couldn't make it, somehow she knew I was not going to let fall to her death. Someone had her back. Someone was going to catch her.

The Manna Principle

There's an awesome story in the Bible that really brings home the reason, why in the midst of our worry we can confidently turn towards God. If you grew up in church you have probably heard lots of stories. Stories are powerful. Stories are one of the easiest ways for us to remember history. Remembering stories from the Bible is extremely important because it reminds us of who God is and how much He pursues us in the midst of our cluttered lives.

When I was a children's pastor in the 90's one of my favorite lessons to teach kids was in Exodus. This story begins in Exodus chapter 16. Of all the stories you have likely heard, this is one of those you should commit to memory, especially if one of your pieces of clutter is worry. The story is about the Israelites collective worry about being able to survive out in the desert. They started whining to Moses, Aaron and God about not having any food. God said He would provide them with something called manna in the morning and quail at night. Manna means, "What is it", because they didn't know what it was at first. The manna principle really has nothing to do with the food. As you will see, it has everything to do with confidence in God when we are drowning in worry.

God Hears You Loud And Clear!

Do you ever wonder if God really hears your cries in the middle of the night? Especially when your are drowning in a sea of worry and fear? When you feel like you're at the end of your rope. Even when you are grumbling, complaining and whining? Does God listen? Moses had a challenge. God had chosen him to lead a couple million people out of slavery in Egypt and relocate them in the promised land. Sounds simple enough. Except for the fact that the whole community of Israel had this clutter in their lives known as "worry".

Exodus 16:1-3 (NLT)

1 Then the whole community of Israel set out from Elim and journeyed into the wilderness of Sin, between Elim and Mount Sinai. They arrived there on the fifteenth day of the second month, one month after leaving the land of Egypt.

2 There, too, the whole community of Israel complained about Moses and Aaron.

3 "If only the Lord had killed us back in Egypt," they moaned. "There we sat around pots filled

with meat and ate all the bread we wanted. But now you have brought us into this wilderness to starve us all to death."

Does that sound like worry to you? Does that sound like the Israelites are focused on the future? It's so bad, that they wanted to revisit their past and become slaves again! However, in the midst of their worry, God was listening!

Exodus 16:11-12 (NLT)
11 Then the Lord said to Moses,
12 "I have heard the Israelites' complaints. Now tell them, 'In the evening you will have meat to eat, and in the morning you will have all the bread you want. Then you will know that I am the Lord your God.'"

If you like to write in your Bible I would circle the words, "I have heard". Every time God says He "hears" watch out, because something is about to happen. If God heard the cries of the Israelites who actually saw the miracles we read about, He will hear your cries. God isn't looking for the right words. God is always looking for a sincere, and sometimes broken, heart. It's always a heart issue! Even in the midst of worry, whining and complaining, God will listen. Why? Because He is a God who hears our cries, every time He hears, He acts.

Before we get to the actual manna part of this story. It's also important to realize that God not only heard the cries of the Israelites but He wanted to intervene and provide for their needs, even though it seemed like impossible odds! Millions of people in the middle of the desert and no fast food joints as far as the eye could see. God prefers the impossible and He knows how He's going to meet our needs long before we do.

Moreover, God also wanted to remind the Israelites that He had never abandoned them. That's one of the reasons for the pillar of fire during the night and the pillar of cloud during the day. It was a visual representation of an invisible truth. God is with us no matter where we are. When you are in the midst of your worry, God hasn't abandoned you. In fact, He has never left your side.

Finally, God was about to test the Israelites in the midst of their worry. This is the part we often miss. It's the part that reveals the most about us to God. Like I said earlier, God knows we're going to worry, but in the midst of our worry is a test. It's not like a spelling test you take in school. It's more of test that would take place during World War II and you were out of ammunition and the Nazis were baring down. Were you a traitor pretending to follow the leader?

All through history, traitors have come in all shapes and sizes. Think about what a traitor does. They say all the right things, look the part and do exactly what you would expect someone who is on your side to do. But, again it's a heart issue. At the core, a traitor is only pretending so they can get what they want. Once that happens they are gone! And if it starts to get really dangerous or out of control they bail.

As we will soon see, this test wasn't even about the food. God knew they needed food. In fact He already knew how He was going to provide it. When they were whining and complaining they weren't telling Him anything He didn't already know. They weren't giving Him any new information. Let's pick back up in Exodus and find out why God provided for the Israelites.

Exodus 16:4 (NLT)
4 Then the Lord said to Moses, "Look, I'm going to rain down food from heaven for you. Each day the people can go out and pick up as much food as they need for that day. I will test them in this to see whether or not they will follow my instructions.

Again, I encourage you to underline the words, "I will test them". God knew He was going to provide for them. But, there was more at stake than just meeting their physical needs. There was a *heart issue* that God wanted to find out about. Every time we start worrying it is more than just the unknown. There is a battle of the heart taking place. Forty years later God brought up this very incident again to Moses.

Deuteronomy 8:2-3 (NLT)

2 Remember how the Lord your God led you through the wilderness for these forty years, humbling you and testing you to prove your character, and to find out whether or not you would obey his commands. 3 Yes, he humbled you by letting you go hungry and then feeding you with manna, a food previously unknown to you and your ancestors. He did it to teach you that people do not live by bread alone; rather, we live by every word that comes from the mouth of the Lord.

God was testing the Israelites. He had a lesson He wanted them to learn in the midst of the test. He wanted to find out if their allegiance to Him was just words. He wanted to know, if push came to shove, if they really did trust Him and were ready to obey Him no matter what. The manna principle includes two parts to this test.

Part one has to do with where our focus is when we are worrying. Is it on what we are worrying about, or on the One who really hears, cares and provides?

The second part of this test is found in the next part of the story. It's the key to unlocking the manna principle in your life. If you embrace this, it will help you to start cleaning out the clutter of worry in your life and replace it with peace.

Exodus 16:16-20 (NLT)

16 These are the Lord's instructions: Each household should gather as much as it needs. Pick up two quarts for each person in your tent."

17 So the people of Israel did as they were told. Some gathered a lot, some only a little.

18 But when they measured it out, everyone had just enough. Those who gathered a lot had nothing left over, and those who gathered only a little had enough. Each family had just what it needed.

19 Then Moses told them, "Do not keep any of it until morning."

20 But some of them didn't listen and kept some of it until morning. But by then it was full of maggots and had a terrible smell. Moses was very angry with them.

Underline, "Each family had just what it needed." This is the lesson He was trying to teach the Israelites, and it's the lesson He is wants to teach you and me. This has changed me in a profound way! Especially in our culture of getting everything you can, when you can, and if you don't you are doomed. God knows us so well. He knows when we have all we need, our hearts start to focus on our provision instead of our provider. Our hearts don't move back to the provider until our provision starts to run out.

What God wants us to understand is that it's about a relationship with Him. He knows exactly what we need and when we need it. When we are in the midst of our worry fest, God is sitting back waiting to see if we will turn to it over to Him and trust Him to provide for us today. Not tomorrow, or a year from now, but today. That's what He promises. That's the second part of the test. That's the key!

God promises me enough for today alone!

In fact some of the Israelites tried to stock pile the manna so they wouldn't run out, or just to have extra. But, every time they did, it would rot and smell up their tent. To even bring home the point more that God can meet our needs, on Saturday they could collect twice as much because on Sunday God wanted them to enjoy each other and Him, instead of worrying about gathering their meal. It didn't rot. Again, **it's not about the provision, it about the provider.** God wants to teach you and me that He promises to meet our needs for today. Jesus echoed this principle in Matthew Chapter 6. Like Father, like Son!

Matthew 6:33-34 (NLT)
33 Seek the Kingdom of God above all else, and live righteously, and he will give you everything you need.
34 "So don't worry about tomorrow, for tomorrow will bring its own worries. Today's trouble is enough for today.

When you and I start to live our lives this way, it drives us back to God every single day. He knows exactly how to provide for your needs. And He knows your needs before you cry out to Him. Through your needs He wants to reveal Himself to you and reassure you that He hears you and wants to provide for you. Remember, it's about a relationship with Him. When I'm worrying, God is asking me... "Am I enough?"

When Kelly and I reached the top of Half Dome, we walked to the edge and gazed at what was before us, we were both speechless. We both said at almost the same time, "It was worth it." God is asking you and I, "Am I worth putting your trust and faith in?"

Top of Half Dome

Chapter 4

Unforgiveness

"Forgiveness is not always easy. At times, it feels more painful than the wound we suffered, to forgive the one that inflicted pain. And yet, there is no peace without forgiveness."
Marianne Williamson

Did you ever have one of those light bulb moments? Maybe you were trapped in an addiction and one day you told yourself, "I don't have to live this way anymore". Maybe you were struggling with an abusive relationship and one day you decide, "I don't have to allow this abuse any more". Or maybe you step on the scale and decide once and for all, "I don't have to be overweight anymore". Something clicks. Everything becomes clear. At that moment, you have attained self-awareness at a deep level.

This piece of clutter is extremely personal to me. This is one of hardest chapters for me to write and I did wrestle with whether or not I was going to include it. But for my sake and yours I felt compelled to. Just as the apostle Paul told the Colossians, who were new to this whole Jesus thing, that he was praying for them.

Colossians 1:9 (NLT)
9 So we have not stopped praying for you since we first heard about you. We ask God to give you complete knowledge of his will and to give you spiritual wisdom and understanding.

My prayer is that as you read this chapter, a light bulb will come on and something is going to click that has been holding you captive, maybe for years. My hope is that you will have the kind of spiritual wisdom and understanding that will free you once and for all from unforgiveness.

Anger and Abuse

What do the following objects all have in common?
Belt
Spatula
Car cigarette lighter
Hot Light bulb
Coat hanger

These are just some of the things my mom used to "discipline" me with. I think a better way to put it is, these are the things she used to take her anger out on me with. My closet was my hiding place when I was growing up. Any time I knew my mom was angry about something I would run to the closet to hide.

I remember one day she was in one of her "moods". I think we were getting ready to eat supper and I was bringing a glass of Kool-Aid over to the table and I dropped it on the new kitchen carpet. (I would love to have a few words with the guy that invented kitchen carpet! It caused me a lot of grief growing up!) As soon as the glass hit the floor I felt her hand grab my arm. As she dragged me to my bed room, profanities flew from her mouth and I knew that whatever she could get her hands on would be the instrument of "discipline". This time is was a hanger. She quickly folded the hanger in half, held down my arm, and with every word she came down hard. "DON'T - EVER - DO - THAT - AGAIN!"

I actually began to hate and fear my mom. The physical abuse finally stopped when I got too big for her to handle. But, the emotional scars remained. I never really told anybody about the abuse for fear of what my mom would do.

Here's my question?

How in the world do you forgive someone who abused you most of your life and taught you that you don't deserve to have a voice? Someone who taught you it's unreasonable for you to express your needs.

I had no plans to ever forgive my mom.

Then in August of 1979 I came face to face with the fact that Jesus loved me enough to give His life for me.

I became a Christ follower. I thought, well now things will get better between my mom and I. Every time I saw my mom, every time I talked to her on the phone an emotion would well up inside of me like a festering volcano. All the memories would come flooding back. I would fight them every way I knew how, but they would still come blasting to the surface. I would wonder, "Why is this so hard? Why can't I just get over this?" I thought, "through Jesus I could do all things." Including forgive my mom. But it didn't happen.

My unforgiveness lasted for another 30 years.

For some of you reading this book, like me, unforgiveness is your number one piece of clutter. Either towards someone else or towards yourself. To say this held me hostage for 40 years is an understatement! It affected my marriage, my ministry, my friendship and my relationship with God.

The Breakthrough

Six months before my mom died, something clicked. The light came on for me in a way that has forever changed my perspective on forgiveness.

Before we get too far into this I think it's very important that I include what forgiveness is not. In our Christian subculture we buy into some pretty sloppy explanations of God's word, especially when it comes to the whole area of forgiveness.

Forgiveness is not…

1. Approving of or diminishing the sin. What my mom did to me was abuse. Period.
2. Enabling the sin. Letting my mom continue the abuse was wrong!
3. Denying the wrong done. What my mom did to me was wrong. Period
4. Waiting for an apology. My mom never apologized for the abuse.
5. Forgetting. I will never forget the things my mom did to me!
6. Ceasing to feel the pain. Every time I think about it, it hurts.
7. A onetime event. I've had to revisit forgiveness towards my mom numerous times.
8. Neglecting justice. If I knew then, what I know now, I would have…
9. Trusting. I never left my mom alone with my kids. Ever!
10. Reconciliation. It takes two people to reconcile. My mom never did.

True Forgiveness

So, what does true forgiveness look like? How could I forgive someone who robbed me of so much? How could I clean out this kind of clutter? One of the reasons I love God's word, is because it addresses these kinds of questions and presents us with real answers. There is an awesome exchange between Peter and Jesus. During this conversation, Peter asks Jesus the same question I asked God over and over again. I love how Jesus answers Peter's question with a story.

Matthew 18:21-27 (NLT)
21 Then Peter came to him and asked, "Lord, how often should I forgive someone who sins against me? Seven times?"
22 "No, not seven times," Jesus replied, "but seventy times seven!
23 "Therefore, the Kingdom of Heaven can be compared to a king who decided to bring his accounts up to date with servants who had borrowed money from him.
24 In the process, one of his debtors was brought in who owed him millions of dollars.
25 He couldn't pay, so his master ordered that he be sold—along with his wife, his children, and everything he owned—to pay the debt.
26 "But the man fell down before his master and begged him, 'Please, be patient with me, and I will pay it all.'
27 Then his master was filled with pity for him, and he released him and forgave his debt.

Stop! I want you to think about all the money you owe right now. All of it. Mortgage, credit cards, car loans, utility bills, school loans and other debts. Now imagine if you were to get a letter in the mail from a place that keeps track of all that stuff. You open up the letter and it looks like a normal bill except all the money you owe is on the bill. Everything is itemized down to the penny.

Statement Of Account
Everything You Owe!

	Universal Debt	$$$/7893
	Account Type	Owner
	SSN/Fed Id	******9999

Code	Account Name	Description	Balance
98340	Mortgage	The place where you live.	249,000
89495	Car loan	That really nice car you couldn't afford	34,000
14534	Utilities	Better get on a budget plan!	500
23435	School loan	You've been paying on these forever dude!	45,000
75939	Hospital visits	That's what weekend athletes get.	5,000
39498	Internet	What you use to check facebook once a weekTot.T	70
94984	Cable TV	Lots of channels, nothing to watch.	75
92234	Phone	Had to have the newest version	300
02039	Your neighbor	Borrowed it last week	50
48593	Your friend Bob	Lent you money for lunch last week	17

Continued on next the page...

I remember when we had our third child, Hannah, we had no insurance. When we got the bill, six pages worth, I almost fainted! We got charged for everything. Cotton pads, meals, bottled water, booties and even the little Band-Aids they put on Hannah's tiny feet. I mean, it just went on and on!

So you get this bill, which is two pages long! You view the first page. Reluctantly, you glance at the second page. And you take a second look! You blink a couple of times to make sure your eyes are really seeing straight. On the second page is the rest of what you owe, only in big bold letters are the words...PAID IN FULL!

Patrick Cannon

Statement Of Account
Everything You Owe!

Universal Debt	$$$/7893
Account Type	Owner
SSN/Fed Id	******9999

Code	Account Name	Description	Balance
74838	Credit card	It's only the minimum payment!	32,000
47282	Dentist	I should brush more.	1,500
83482	Computers R Us	That laptop was my sweet ball!	700
		Total	685412
		Balance Due	0

PAID IN FULL

Imagine how you would feel! It would be just like winning the lottery! That's exactly how the guy in this story should feel. There was no way he could ever repay his debt and now the slate is clean. If Jesus would have stopped there the story would have been a great example of forgiveness. As usual though, Jesus digs deeper.

Matthew 18:28-35 (NLT)
28 "But when the man left the king, he went to a fellow servant who owed him a few thousand dollars. He grabbed him by the throat and demanded instant payment.
29 "His fellow servant fell down before him and begged for a little more time. 'Be patient with me, and I will pay it,' he pleaded.
30 But his creditor wouldn't wait. He had the man arrested and put in prison until the debt could be paid in full.

Right after this guy gets his life back and has his debt forgiven, he refuses to forgive someone else's debt. It's crazy how fast we forget, isn't it?

31 "When some of the other servants saw this, they were very upset. They went to the king and told him everything that had happened.
32 Then the king called in the man he had forgiven and said, 'You evil servant! I forgave you that tremendous debt because you pleaded with me.
33 Shouldn't you have mercy on your fellow servant, just as I had mercy on you?'
34 Then the angry king sent the man to prison to be tortured until he had paid his entire debt.
35 "That's what my heavenly Father will do to you if you refuse to forgive your brothers and sisters from your heart."

When I first read verse 35, I stopped and read again a couple times. At first I thought, "wait a second. I've placed my faith in Jesus. The Bible says I'm sealed. No one can take that away. What is Jesus saying here? My debt won't be forgiven. I thought Jesus paid my debt?"

Read it one more time

What I believe Jesus is saying to you and me is this:

When we choose not to forgive we become prisoners.

Remember clutter causes confusion, chaos and captivity. When we choose not to forgive we are actually being held hostage. This comes out in lots of ways; bottled up anger, bitterness and depression. I had become a prisoner of all the things my mom had done to me. I had let it lock me up. In prison you are only allowed to do what the guards tell you to do. When you become a prisoner of unforgiveness, you are only allowed to do as much as your past lets you do. Your emotions are locked down, the way you relate to others is locked down and your future is locked down.

Here's the second truth that helped the light bulb to come on for me. In the story we just read, what was the unforgiving servant's number one thing that prevented him from showing forgiveness to his friend? Look at verse 27 again...

Matthew 18:27 (NLT)
27 Then his master was filled with pity for him, and he released him and forgave his debt.

He forgot about the great debt that was forgiven Him! This was the second piece to the puzzle I needed in order to move towards forgiving my mom.

Forgiveness is when I tell someone else or myself, they no longer owe me anything.

As a Christ follower this should be easy for us to do. But it's not. I really think the reason why is that we don't grasp just how much Jesus forgave us. Maybe at this point in the book you're thinking, "yeah yeah I should forgive, but I still need some more convincing." Let's say you received another bill in the mail and this time instead of all the money you owe it has all the sins you have every committed up to this very moment. From the day you were born until this very second. Every sin spelled out in graphic detail. What your heart motivation was. Why it grieved the heart of God and how it affected those around you. For all of us it wouldn't arrive in an envelope but in one of these. A big dump truck.

Let's be honest. If it takes a dump truck to just carry your sin, imagine what it would take to deliver the entire planet's sin bill! We are all dead, lost and without hope. All of us have a huge debt called sin that needs to be paid. Fortunately for you and me, God already had an amazing plan. A plan to pay our debt.

Ephesians 4:32 (NLT)
32 Instead, be kind to each other, tenderhearted, forgiving one another, just as God through Christ has forgiven you.

That was the final piece to the puzzle for me.

I must forgive like Jesus forgave me.

Then it clicked. The lights came on. Was my mom less deserving of forgiveness than I was? Did my mom's actions somehow over shadow my sin and make me more worthy to be forgiven than her? No. Was it wrong for my mom to abuse me the way she did? Absolutely. But, her abuse no longer had to hold me hostage. The only way to release its grip was through forgiveness.

I came to grip with three facts:

1. I was a prisoner.
2. The only way for me to become free was to let my mom know she no longer owed me anything.
3. My forgiveness needed to mirror the forgiveness of Jesus.

I knew I had to take the next step. What about you? Is there someone that is holding you hostage because you are refusing to forgive him or her? It's no skin off their back and it could cost you everything. What are the next steps? For me it was an exercise that a counselor friend of mine helped me do. I actually did this six months before my mom passed away in a little hospital in Ogallala, Nebraska.

Step One
Clearly identify who you need to forgive. In the case of my mom it was very easy. For you it might take a little work. The best way to figure it out is to think about the those imaginary conversations you have about someone. You know, where you verbally take them apart piece by piece. You let them know everything they did wrong and how totally evil they are. They in turn leave sputtering, unable to answer your righteous anger. Those that are watching you during this imaginary conversation are cheering you on and clapping. Finally at the end the person who you're mad at comes crawling on their knees begging for forgiveness. *Those are the people you need to forgive.*

Step Two
Get out a sheet of paper and actually write down everything they took from you. I mean everything. Your childhood. Your money. Your job. Your reputation. Your freedom. Your voice. Your innocence. Your marriage. Your future. I can't stress how important it is that you are very specific.

Step Three
Now fold up the sheet of paper, stick it in an envelope and seal it up. On the front of the envelope write the words. "THEY DON'T OWE ME ANY MORE"

I don't want to in any way, shape, or form, paint the picture that this was easy for me to do. In fact, I would encourage you to do this with a trusted friend or your pastor. You will need their support. After you are done, destroy the envelope in whatever way you want. I took mine home for a few days and then went in my back yard and burned it. As I watched the flames consume it something took place inside of me. The weight of carrying unforgiveness for 40 years began to lift. Over the next month I actually began to feel sorry for my mom. I even booked a flight and took my youngest daughter, whom she had never met, with me to visit my mom in the hospital. The moment I walked into her room I experienced something brand new with my mom. I felt compassion for her. Here was this shell of a woman, the one that had caused so much pain in my life, and I no longer hated her. I knew only the power of forgiveness could make me feel the way I did. I introduced her to my daughter and we talked about a few things. She was on so many medications, she would slip in and out of conversations. Towards the end of our visit we were getting ready to leave. I remember looking at my mom, giving her a hug and telling her I loved her. This time I really meant it. Little did I know that only two weeks later she would die. This journey of finding forgiveness was a long road for me. I wish I could tell you there weren't days that I have flash backs of the beatings I received at the hands of my mom. There are. I have spent hours in counseling gaining back my voice. Now when I talk about my mom those volcano like emotions no longer want to erupt. They have been replaced with compassion and forgiveness. Remember, forgiveness isn't only for the other person. It's for you!

Colossians 3:13 (NLT)
13 Make allowance for each other's faults, and forgive anyone who offends you. Remember, the Lord forgave you, so you must forgive others.

Chapter 5

Fear

"I have told you all this so that you may have peace in me. Here on earth you will have many trials and sorrows. But take heart, because I have overcome the world."
Jesus Christ

A few years ago there was a ten-part mini-series produced by Tom Hanks, Steven Spielberg, and Gary Goetzman on World War II titled, The Pacific. This series focused mainly on what took place in the Pacific, between Japan and the United States. The series followed the lives of specific individuals. One individual, who I will call "Red", desperately wanted to fight in the war, but because of some medical issues he was continually turned down. Red had a romantic idea, as many young men did, of what fighting in the war would be like. The more he saw his friends and own family members get drafted, the more desperate he became to fight, until finally through the help of his dad, his wish came true. He had a romantic idea, as many young men did, of what fighting in the war would be like.

The one scene that stands out for me is when he is about to experience war first hand. Roughly 30 soldiers are standing in a landing craft as it is still in one of the big battle ships. WWII landing craft were all flat-bottomed, with many designs also having a flat front, a lower able ramp, instead of a normal bow. These ships were specifically designed to carry infantry into battle. There's barely any light until the huge ramp lowers. There is a close-up of Red. You can feel the anticipation of, "oh yeah I finally get to go into the battle!" As the huge ramp lowers the scene is invaded by sunlight. As the landing craft is launched the reality of the battle becomes clear. The engines roar. Machine guns fire. Explosions are everywhere. Then the camera pans to various soldiers in the craft. One is throwing up; another is staring out into space. Red's expression slowly changes from a slight smile to fear. All of a sudden the reality of the battle hits home. As Red begins to pray the sergeant barks out the orders, "load and lock gentlemen"!

As I was watching this scene it reminded me of the experience that many of us have when we first become Christ followers. We have this "romantic idea" about what following Jesus will be like. We listen to inspiring communicators, read books about individuals who did "great things" for God. Then we start to imagine doing "great things" for God. We just want to get into the battle! Little did we know that as soon as that ramp lowers we come face to face with the reality of following Jesus and what the battle will require. Red came face to face with one of the most debilitating pieces of clutter that can collect in our lives. FEAR.

We are close to celebrating our fourth year as a church in one of the most impoverished, and dangerous areas in Toledo. Since I have been here, I have had to walk up and step through the door called fear almost every week. All of us have things that make us fearful. You know when this door becomes really big? When we experience situations that we can't handle. Remember that old saying? "God will not put on you.....(I bet you can finish it). Aside from sounding really good and spiritual, that saying only has one problem. It's not Biblical! I used to hang my hat on that saying. I used to counsel other people with that saying. Until I moved down into our neighborhood. There's always some "well meaning" Christian brother or sister who always brings up one specific verse...

1 Corinthians 10:13 (NLT)
13 The temptations in your life are no different from what others experience. And God is faithful. He will not allow the temptation to be more than you can stand. When you are tempted, he will show you a way out so that you can endure.

The reality of this verse is that Paul is talking about facing temptations, not life circumstances. Being tempted by our own lust or by someone or something else is one thing; facing overwhelming circumstances is another. We have to be very careful not to take scripture and make it say what we want it to say. The same guy that wrote this verse, Paul, also has something to say about facing life circumstances. In his second letter to the same church, Paul wanted to make it very clear that sometimes we are pushed to the brink of despair. Wait, you mean Paul? Paul? The one we put on a pedestal as "Mr. Spiritual"? The one who used rocks for pillows? The one who confronted fellow disciples face-to-face and called them on the carpet about various issues? That Paul? Yep. Read the following verse:

2 Corinthians 1:8 (NIV)
8 We do not want you to be uninformed, brothers, about the hardships we suffered in the province

of Asia. We were under great pressure, far beyond our ability to endure, so that we despaired even of life.

Wow! Now that's pressure! Paul is saying that he was pushed far beyond his ability to endure. In other words, he couldn't handle it!

Have you ever been there? Over the last three years there have been many circumstances that I felt I couldn't handle. My "fear door" became huge! Maybe that's where you are today. You are at the point in your life where you feel like you can't handle it any more. Your fear door is staring you in the face. Maybe you recently had a conversation with God that went something like this:

"God, I can't handle this anymore! I'm ready to give up!"
"My marriage is a mess and I don't know if I will survive it!"
"My daughter is out of control and I'm clueless as to what to do next!"
"If I don't get a job soon, we'll lose our house!"
"The doctors can't do anything else for me!"

I've had some of those same conversations. How in the world do you get to the door called fear and have the courage to open it up and step through? What I love about God's word is that He doesn't leave us stranded outside of our fear door. God's word is filled with those that faced overwhelming circumstances and though they didn't become fearless, they were able to open their fear door and walk through.

One of my favorite stories about cleaning up the fear clutter is about a king that faced overwhelming circumstances and found the courage to face his biggest fears. He didn't become fearless. He discovered the secret to conquering his fear.

The king's name is Jehoshapat. (I bet he got teased in school!) Anyway, King Jehoshaphat started off wanting to seek after God.

2 Chronicles 17:3-4 (NLT)
3 The Lord was with Jehoshaphat because he followed the example of his father's early years and did not worship the images of Baal.
4 He sought his father's God and obeyed his commands instead of following the evil practices of the kingdom of Israel.

The whole kingdom of Judah praised Jehoshaphat. Even though he didn't do everything right, God knew his heart and the kingdom of Judah began to prosper. Everything seemed to be going well until we get to Chapter 20. Then, BAM! Everything goes south!

2 Chronicles 20:1 (NLT)
1 After this, the armies of the Moabites, Ammonites, and some of the Meunites declared war on Jehoshaphat.

This was huge. Not only had God been blessing the nation of Judah, but He had been protecting them from being attacked. All of a sudden, out of nowhere, bam! That's what happens sometimes. You get that phone call, you receive that medical report or get that pink slip. Out of nowhere you become overwhelmed.

Last summer we had just finished a Saturday night service. Everything had gone pretty well. We were starting to clean up when someone ran in the door and grabbed my arm screaming. "There's a big fight two blocks down and Justin has a bat"! My door just grew from 10 to 30 feet high! I went running down the street and sure enough there was Justin with a steel bat in his hand. His mom was on top of him trying to hold him down. The other guy he wanted to fight took his shirt off. When guys take their shirts off in our neighborhood you know something bad is about to happen. My door continued to grow another 20 feet! I didn't remember reading in my pastor's handbook how to wrestle bats away from anybody so I just jumped in. Arms flailing, legs kicking! I finally grabbed the bat. Another guy came up to hold Justin down. After about a minute the whole thing was over.

I never saw it coming. Maybe that's where you are at right now. You never saw it coming. That's when problems come. We never see it coming and all of a sudden you're in over your head.

2 Chronicles 20:2 (NLT)
2 Messengers came and told Jehoshaphat, "A vast army from Edom is marching against you from beyond the Dead Sea. They are already at Hazazon-tamar." (This was another name for En-gedi.)

Imagine how Jehoshaphat felt when these guys rode up, jumped off their horses out of breath and told him that not only is there a huge army on their way to attack him, they are at his back door! Jehoshaphat had no time to think about strategy or plan a counter offensive. His fear door had expanded way beyond his ability to handle it. His reaction was similar to ours when we are overwhelmed.

2 Chronicles 20:3-4 (NLT)
3 Jehoshaphat was terrified by this news and begged the Lord for guidance. He also ordered everyone in Judah to begin fasting.
4 So people from all the towns of Judah came to Jerusalem to seek the Lord's help.

I feel like I have been at this place more than I care to admit, when I have been so overwhelmed and fearful that my prayers become nothing more than begging. Not only did it drive Jehoshaphat to his knees, but it drove the whole nation to its knees! No messing around, start fasting, now! Not only was Jehoshaphat overwhelmed, but the whole nation was.

The crazy thing is that I used to think I should always know what to do. I thought as a Christian you should always know what to do, especially when you're overwhelmed. Just quote Philippians 4:13, "I can do all things through Christ who strengthens me", and all will be well. We have bought into this, "God will not put more on you than you can handle" hook line and sinker. If you don't know what to do, "you don't have enough faith". The craziest thing about that lie is it is not in the Bible! Anywhere! Let's jump to verse 12. Remember Jehoshaphat has been trying to follow God up to this point.

2 Chronicles 20:12 (NLT)
12 O our God, won't you stop them? We are powerless against this mighty army that is about to attack us. We do not know what to do, but we are looking to you for help."

From the time we opened That Neighborhood Church, almost every week, that's exactly how I feel. I am powerless against this "mighty army" that is attacking our neighborhood. I don't know what to do. Every problem we face is huge! There are many times during our leadership team meetings when we look at each other and admit we have no clue what the next steps are.

What's the first step in moving toward your fear door?

Let God know you are over your head and you don't know what to do.

When I finally admitted that to myself and to God it did something I never expected; it made me stop boasting about what I can do and made me desperate for what God can do. Let me ask you a question. When was the last time you were desperate for God? I mean really desperate. Like, "God if you don't come through I am sunk", desperate. Over the past three years my desperation for God has increased 10 fold.

From the time we opened That Neighborhood Church, our main focus has been to follow God's lead no matter where it took us. I'll let you in on a little secret. When you plan on following God's lead no matter what, you will be overwhelmed. I guarantee it. God will lead you to places where you have no choice but to trust Him. TNC is a small little church in the middle of the "hood". If we could just concentrate on being this nice little church, with a nice little service every week, a midweek Bible study, and some stuff for the kids that would be great. The only problem is that won't work in urban ministry. In order for inner city ministry to be effective there needs to be two core pieces to the ministry.

Piece #1 - Real Need Ministry. These ministries help meet the tangible needs of our neighbors. It helps provide food, clothes and life skill vocational training.

Piece #2 - Church ministry. This provides a place to worship, gather, children's/youth ministry, and Bible studies.

If you only do #1 you become another social agency without any spiritual power. If you only do #2 you become a noisy gong and clanging cymbal. The gospel becomes irrelevant. You need both and we don't have much money? About 95% of our budget is met through the gifts of those outside of our neighborhood. Don't get me wrong, our neighbors tithe, but it's like the widow's mite.

Let me ask you a question. What is your "normal"? By normal, I mean, the things you do every day without even thinking about it. It's how you live every day. You make your decisions based on your "normal". You create goals based on your "normal". How you raise your kids is based on your "normal". How you treat other people is based on your "normal". Where did your "normal" come from? Most likely, it was taught to you.

Our "normal" can either be good or toxic. The "normal" down in the '04, it's the last two digits of our zip code in our neighborhood, is quite different than in suburbia. It's normal down in the '04 for kids not to know who their father is or even see him. It's normal down in the '04 for kids to not graduate. It's normal down in the '04 for 7 year olds to wonder the neighborhood at 11 at night. It's normal for kids to be alone all day without any parental involvement. It's normal for drugs to be bought and sold on the streets. It's normal for girls and women to sell themselves just to pay the rent. It's normal to not have an ingrained work ethic. It's normal to steal from others. It's normal to gain respect by being able to fight and impregnate as many women as you can. It's normal to pay $500-$600 a month for rat infested places to live. It's normal to feel oppressed and without hope.

The only way for God to change the toxic "normal" into a healthy "normal" is to start with the basics. God has led us to open up a number of bridge building real need ministries to help meet physical needs while building relationships. Here are just a few...

Rahab's Heart
This ministry targets women trapped in adult prostitution. Street outreach and groups are already taking place and we are hoping to have the Rahab's Heart drop in center renovations done this year.

That Neighborhood Free Health Clinic
Lack of quality health care in our neighborhood is a huge problem. For over a year and a half this clinic has been in the planning stages. This last January That Neighborhood Free Health Clinic officially opened its doors at the local YMCA. The cost for running the clinic and volunteers needed is overwhelming.

That Neighborhood Vocational Center
Second and third generation "generational poverty" has created something very toxic in our neighborhood. It has robbed our neighbors of an ingrained work ethic and the knowledge of basic life skills. That

Neighborhood Vocational Center will teach basic automotive mechanical skills along with life skills and other vocational training. Not only did God raise the building, but He provided all the money to purchase it with cash. Renovations will start this summer. We are hoping to start car care clinics this coming fall. This will take tons of volunteers and money to become a reality.

Talk about being overwhelmed! When God started leading us in these directions my fear door became the size of the Gate of Mordor from Lord of the Rings! How is all this going to happen? I still have no idea. But, it led me to do what the whole nation of Judah did.

2 Chronicles 20:13 (NLT)
13 As all the men of Judah stood before the Lord with their little ones, wives, and children,

When the entire nation of Judah was overwhelmed with fear they did what God calls us to do today.

Seek God!

God has used these last three years to drive me to my knees, plant my face to the ground and desperately seek Him. Seek Him for answers, seek Him for courage, seek Him for endurance and seek Him for peace. When was the last time you were face-down, on the floor before God seeking Him? Our leadership team meets twice a month. Before we do anything we spend time praying. Sometimes there are tears. Sometimes we just sit in silence waiting for God's direction. Every one of us knows that if God doesn't come through we are sunk!

As the entire nation of Judah was seeking God, someone followed God's lead to speak the truth. It was this truth that propelled Judah forward. It was this truth that gave them the courage to not only walk up to their fear door, but open it up and step through it.

2 Chronicles 20:14-15 (NLT)
14 the Spirit of the Lord came upon one of the men standing there. His name was Jahaziel son of Zechariah, son of Benaiah, son of Jeiel, son of Mattaniah, a Levite who was a descendant of Asaph. 15 He said, "Listen, all you people of Judah and Jerusalem! Listen, King Jehoshaphat!

STOP! If you're like me, you tend to read through passages like this way to fast! If you like to underline stuff in your Bible, underline the word "listen". Many times when we are full of fear and feeling overwhelmed, listening is one of the best things we can do. That's when God is trying to say something to you. Don't waste it! What Jahaziel said next was the one thing that not only gave the entire nation of Judah courage, but it has given me the courage to open my fear door and walk through it.

2 Chronicles 20:15 (NLT)
15 He said, "Listen, all you people of Judah and Jerusalem! Listen, King Jehoshaphat! This is

what the Lord says: Do not be afraid! Don't be discouraged by this mighty army, for the battle is not yours, but God's.

When I started to grasp this truth, my ability to not only face my fear, but actually embrace it, started to grow. The battle raging down in the '04 isn't mine, it's God's. The battle for raising money and volunteers isn't mine, it's God's. All He asks me to do is follow His lead the best way I can, the results are up to Him. What is the "mighty army" in your life right now? What label would you put on your fear door? This wasn't only a "truth" that gave the whole nation of Judah to ability to face their mighty army with courage, it's a truth that can change how you deal with your fears!

Realize the battle is not mine, but God's

Remember the verse we started with at the beginning of this chapter (2 Corinthians 1:8)? Paul wanted the Corinthian church to know about how hard it has been for him. Verse 9 ties it all together. I can tell you that my experience over these last three years has proven this truth over and over. Do you ever wonder why God even allows us to become overwhelmed? Why He wants us to face our fears head on? Read on...

2 Corinthians 1:8-9 (NLT)
8 We think you ought to know, dear brothers and sisters, about the trouble we went through in the province of Asia. We were crushed and

overwhelmed beyond our ability to endure, and we thought we would never live through it.

9 In fact, we expected to die. But as a result, *we stopped relying on ourselves* and *learned to rely only on God,* who raises the dead.

I am learning how to stop *relying on myself* and how to *rely on God.* But, that didn't happen until I decided to face my fears. Learning how to rely on God doesn't just happen. We have to get to the point in our lives where there is no other option but to rely on God.

Yeah, yeah. I can hear some very well intentioned people saying, "You should be relying on God all the time, not just when your overwhelmed". That sounds nice and super spiritual, but in my experience we can't say we rely on God until we face circumstances that overwhelm us. That's when the truth of our reliance on God comes to the surface.

I want to end this chapter with a challenge. Take out a sheet of paper and write out the number one fear in your life right now. Make it as large as you can. Tack it or tape it to the inside of your bedroom door. Every time you leave your room ask God to give you the courage to face that fear. Then take the next steps to overcome it. Make that appointment, call, or have that conversation. When you stop relying on yourself and start relying on God, that's when you will find the courage to face your fear.

Chapter 6

Anger

"Anger is an acid that can do more harm to the vessel in which it is stored than to anything on which it is poured"
Mark Twain

The Beast Within!

When I was growing up I loved watching monster movies! In our town we had a show called "Creature Feature" that was on late at night on Saturday. On those nights I would try to convince my older brothers to let me watch it instead of "Don Kirchner's Rock Concert". Sometimes I would win! One of my favorites was Dr. Jekyll and Mr. Hyde, the story about a good doctor trying to figure out how to control the good and evil parts of who he was. On the outside he was a calm, gentle man that everyone admired, but deep within was another side that would come out spewing anger, lust, and murder.

There's another movie about a guy who is exposed to too much gamma radiation. Every time he gets upset, everything come unglued. He turns into a huge green hulk whose only mission is to smash whatever gets in his way.

Even though these are just movies, they portray a very real part of our human experience. Anger.

Before we get too far, I think it's very important to remember where anger came from in the first place. This might seem a little strange at first, but anger actually originated with God. The Bible makes it very clear that God is Holy and that God is love. Nowhere does it say that God is anger. But, because He is perfectly holy and perfectly loving God does experience anger. In fact, the word anger is found 455 times in the Old Testament alone and 375 of these refer to God's anger.

What is amazing about this is that it's God's concern for justice and righteousness, which is born out of His holiness and love that causes God to get angry!

When God sees evil He experiences anger. Anger is His logical response to injustice and sin.

Since we are made in God's image, even though that image was marred by sin after Adam and Eve disobeyed God, His image was not erased. Every human being that is born has an image of God pressed deep into their soul. That's why we get "angry" over injustice. I must admit there is something deep inside of me when I see a man beating up a woman or a child. There is an anger that wells up in me. It's at those times that I wish I was a Mike Tyson.

Even at an early age we start learning toxic ways to express this part of God's image. If any of you have kids you know exactly what I'm talking about, it's called a tantrum. The best ones seem to happen at Walmart! It's all based on one little phrase. "That's not fair"! For my kids it started as soon as they could talk. You know why? Because deep within us is stamped this sense of knowing when we feel wronged or something isn't right. And as all kids do they just say, or scream, what they feel.

I'm going to make a statement that might be a little hard to swallow, but it's Biblically accurate.

Anger itself is not evil. Anger itself is not sinful. Anger did not start with our sinful nature. Anger did not come from Satan.

Anger is evidence that we are made in the image of God. It shows from the deepest core of our being that we still have a concern for justice and righteousness in spite of our sinfulness. It reveals our concern for righteousness, justice and fairness. In fact we should thank God for our ability to experience anger. If we lose our ability to get angry we lose our ability to stand up for what is right.

Godly good anger is designed by God to motivate us to take constructive action in the face of injustice.

There are numerous stories in the Bible where God's anger was about to be poured out on a group of people because of the incredible injustices that were going on. A great example is the story of Jonah. In that story God was going to wipe out an entire city because disobedience and injustice of its citizens was running rampant. God chose to send a guy named Jonah to warn the Ninevites that God had enough. Because Jonah hated the Ninevites, he tried to run from God, but that never works. Jonah ends up becoming lunch for a huge fish, gets puked up on shore next to Ninevah. He proceeds to tell everyone how angry God is and if they don't change their ways, they are toast! Something happens that Jonah never expected, but God knew would occur.

Jonah 3:1-10 (NLT)
1 Then the Lord spoke to Jonah a second time:
2 "Get up and go to the great city of Nineveh, and deliver the message I have given you."
3 This time Jonah obeyed the Lord's command and went to Nineveh, a city so large that it took three days to see it all.
4 On the day Jonah entered the city, he shouted to the crowds: "Forty days from now Nineveh will be destroyed!"
5 The people of Nineveh believed God's message, and from the greatest to the least, they declared a fast and put on burlap to show their sorrow.
6 When the king of Nineveh heard what Jonah was saying, he stepped down from his throne and took

off his royal robes. He dressed himself in burlap and sat on a heap of ashes.

7 Then the king and his nobles sent this decree throughout the city: "No one, not even the animals from your herds and flocks, may eat or drink anything at all.

8 People and animals alike must wear garments of mourning, and everyone must pray earnestly to God. They must turn from their evil ways and stop all their violence.

9 Who can tell? Perhaps even yet God will change his mind and hold back his fierce anger from destroying us."

10 When God saw what they had done and how they had put a stop to their evil ways, he changed his mind and did not carry out the destruction he had threatened.

God's anger was expressed towards the Ninevites not because He hated them but because He loved them. He couldn't allow their injustice and disobedience to continue. As a result, the entire nation changed their way and God's compassion flowed. He chose not to destroy them. God's anger actually served a positive purpose and changed an entire nation.

Our history is filled with individuals whose anger fueled positive changes. People like Martin Luther King Jr., whose anger towards injustice against blacks fueled a fire in his soul that was unquenchable. He began a movement that caused our country to search its soul for God's view of people rather than our own self-righteous views. Beckie Brown, who's 19 year old son was killed by a repeat offender drunk driver in December of 1979, channeled her anger into helping to start Mothers Against Drunk Driving.

Simply stated, anger can be good and righteous. But, as we all know there is also a dark side to anger.

Angry Truth

For someone like me, who can take a lot before getting angry, this kind of clutter was buried deep under many other things. It wasn't until my world came crashing in that this clutter made its way to the surface. I'm not proud of what I'm about to share, but as my toxic anger surfaced I began to learn some very key truths that have helped me keep the beast within at bay.

I'm the kind of person that doesn't get angry very often, but when I do, it's not pretty. I will never forget the day when I exploded in front of my kids for the first time. I was experiencing what I like to describe as the "week of pain and misery." I had just told the former owner of the print shop I was buying, that he could have the shop back. My Honda Civics' engine had melted on the highway. Our water bed exploded. Our washing machine broke and my wife found out she was pregnant with our third child, which she wasn't ready for. I absolutely hate screaming. When I walked in the door that Friday, I heard my wife, who was also at the end of her rope, yelling at our kids. I completely lost it! I began yelling. I put my fist through our living room wall and then went over to our bedroom door and kicked a large hole in it. Yes, this mild mannered Christian man had turned into the red headed hulk. I don't think I turned green. It was more of a red color.

After it was all over, I went into the bedroom, fell on the side of the bed and just started weeping. My mind swirled with various disconnected thoughts. What just happened? Where did that come from? How will my kids view their dad? What is wrong with me? It's out of the bag now! After a good 30 minutes I gathered up my thoughts, blew my nose and walked into the living room. Everyone was silent. I could see the fear in my kids' faces. (That hurt me the most). I fell to my knees and told everyone I was sorry. My youngest son PJ came up to me and said something very profound. "That's ok daddy, I know you're scared".

My little boy communicated the truth about so much of our anger. It's a hidden truth...

Anger is a "warning light" that something deeper is going on. For me, I didn't know just how fearful I was until it surfaced through anger.

When I stopped to unpack why I exploded, I discovered lots of fears and frustrations that had nothing to do with my anger. I was afraid not knowing how we were going to survive financially. I was frustrated with the way my wife was dealing with her emotions. I was confused about why God lead us to buy a business only to see it collapse. The bottom line was I was hurt. Many times, the more we hurt the deeper the anger.

The next time you get angry, ask yourself a simple question: "Why am I angry?"

How you answer that question will determine whether or not your anger is toxic or righteous. Remember anger is a God given emotion. It's not always wrong, but it's not always good either.

As I began to unpack why I had exploded in anger, there were other times I began to think about what was modeled to me growing up. A lot of how we react to things are the result of how those we grew up with reacted to situations. My mom was not only a screamer, but explosive in her anger. Because of her struggle with depression and the medication she was taking, she had extreme ups and downs. It was very "normal" for her to start off the morning humming a song, but by lunch explode with anger over something trivial. This went on for years. What I didn't realize was that I was being taught a toxic way to deal with life through anger. The only problem was I thought it was "normal".

Then there were the times I "lost it" with my brothers. There were four boys in our family. Everyone was skinny, except me. I was "husky". I had freckles, they did not. I wore thick black glasses, they did not. I had red hair, they did not. I wasn't good at sports, they were. I thought I was adopted for the longest time! This all added up to years of typical verbal and physical abuse. I would take it for a while, but because I didn't feel the freedom to voice my hurt and anger, I would let it get to the point of an explosion.

The worst was the time I took a utility knife after my brothers. They laughed at my attempt. I left the house intending never to return. I didn't get very far, because supper was soon and I was getting hungry!

The second truth about anger is that we learn how to express it from others.

So there I was, holding on to this toxic piece of clutter that was causing chaos, confusion and holding me captive. I wish I could tell you once I became a Christ follower this all went away, but my worst outbursts happened after. This would only drive me deeper into depression. I'm supposed to be a new creation in Christ! All things are gone! Behold all things become new! Didn't "all things" mean my anger too? I would pray more. I would have other people pray for me. I looked up all the verses on anger like...

Proverbs 14:29 (NLT)
29 People with understanding control their anger; a hot temper shows great foolishness.

Proverbs 15:1 (NLT)
1 A gentle answer deflects anger, but harsh words make tempers flare.

Ecclesiastes 7:9 (NLT)
9 Control your temper, for anger labels you a fool.

Ephesians 4:26-27 (NLT)
26 And "don't sin by letting anger control you." Don't let the sun go down while you are still angry, 27 for anger gives a foothold to the devil.

It wasn't until my explosion in front of my wife and kids that I decided to create a new "normal" when it comes to expressing my anger. In order to do that I had to take a personal inventory into what was actually going on in my life. Maybe that's where you are today. For you, toxic anger could be one of the pieces of clutter in your life that is causing chaos, confusion and captivity. Whether it's been a part of your "normal" since you can remember or if it's been rearing its ugly head only recently, let me give you a couple of questions to ask yourself. This should help you create what I call an anger profile.

1. Ask yourself...Why am I angry?

This may take a little work. To help you get started answer these questions:

a. What are some of the things I am most afraid of:

> At work?
> With my marriage?
> With my kids?
> With my future?

b. What is it in my life that causes me the most stress? Why?

c. What am I the most disappointed about?

2. What did I see modeled growing up when it comes to anger? Was it toxic or healthy? Why?

What same patterns do I see in my own life?

How you answer these questions should begin to give you a picture of why you express anger the way you do. Once you begin to discover the core of your anger profile it's time to start creating a new "normal". You might be surprised to find out that it has nothing to do with anger as much as it does trust. For me, once I discovered my angry outbursts were birthed out of fear, I began communicating my fear to my wife before I got angry. I began communicating my fear to God on a regular basis. I even communicated my fear to my kids. I confessed to God that I really didn't believe He could take care of me and my family. I was like the man who came to Jesus and asked Him to help him with his unbelief. I was expecting anger and condemnation from God, but like Jesus' reaction to the man, I received grace.

I believe the best way to start cleaning out the clutter of toxic anger in our lives is complete transparency with ourselves, God and those we love. Toxic anger doesn't have to hold you captive. What I have discovered along this journey, which I'm still on by the way, is that my ability to communicate my fears to others and God is directly related to my toxic anger.

Chapter 7

Lust

"God disappears to lust-glazed eyes."
Kent Hughes

Remember that old Budweiser commercial where the main phrase was "This Bud's for you!" Guys, "This chapter is for you!" I'm not saying that women don't struggle with lust, but let's be honest, for most men, the largest piece of clutter we are constantly trying to clean out is lust. Stop and think about all the different things people lust after:

Money
Power
Fame
Control
Sex
Drugs
Alcohol
60" HD TV with surround sound.

That last one is mine. Anyway, the list is endless. In our culture if you mention the word lust where does everybody's mind go? SEX. For guys, this is especially true. Our culture is expert at capitalizing on this piece of clutter. It's used to sell everything from fishing boats to diamonds. It's become a "recreational" activity on TV shows and in movies. You can find it on the internet in two clicks.

This isn't a new concept by any means. In fact, before the internet, TV, or even the printing press, lust has been causing chaos, captivity and confusion in the hearts of men and women. Almost 3,700 years ago God warned the people of Israel about the toxic effects of lust.

Exodus 34:15-17 (NLT)
15 "You must not make a treaty of any kind with the people living in the land. They lust after their gods, offering sacrifices to them. They will invite you to join them in their sacrificial meals, and you will go with them.
16 Then you will accept their daughters, who sacrifice to other gods, as wives for your sons. And they will seduce your sons to commit adultery against me by worshiping other gods.

Lust at Its Core

Lust has at its core idol worship. We hardly if ever hear anyone talk about idol worship in our culture. That's because it's become so accepted and subtle. When's the last time you saw a commercial about a huge golden statute of a cow?

The lights come up. There's some rock in' music in the background. The camera pans around to people in different situations. The announcer says something like, "Are you tired of never having a date? Is your breath creating panic in the streets? Are your eyelashes only a 1/8 of an inch long? Is your car more than 5 years old, repelling chicks instead attracting them? All that can be a thing of the past! All you have to do is bow down and worship this golden calf. It's only takes 10 minutes a day! That's right. Just give it some of your money, time, and energy, and we promise... blah, blah, blah."

How many people would jump at the chance to worship that idol? Not many. Why? Because of the way it's presented. The message has always been the same.

"What you have now is bad, wrong, outdated. What you need and deserve is good, right and new."

It's all based on temporary promises. Will it make me feel good? Yeah, for a little while. Will it give me more confidence? Yeah, for a little while. Will it fill that emptiness deep in my soul? I tell myself it will.

If there's one piece of clutter that has derailed marriages, ministries and families more than anything else its lust. More often than not, hidden within this piece of clutter is an addiction to something I discovered at the age of 10. Both its creation and distribution have increased at least 100 fold since the internet. American's spend more on this addiction than is spent by every professional sports team combined. It brings in more than 13 billion dollars every year. Its internet sales alone brings in more than 3 billion. To get a better picture, that's $354 every second. If you're a guy reading this, you already know what I'm talking about. Pornography.

As someone who was held captive in this addiction for almost 15 years, 5 years of that was after I became a Christ follower, I want to encourage you to read on. Everyone has their own story as to when they were first exposed to porn. Mine happened behind our house. We had little forest that led to the city dump. My brothers and I would venture out to the dump quit often. You never know what you could find. It was during one of these "adventures" that I found my first porn magazine. Of course, I didn't want my brothers to know, so I hid it under some other junk. I knew just where to find it every time we returned. It became my escape. The only place I felt like I could go to get away from my mom's wrath and my brother's non-stop teasing. When I opened that magazine it was as if I entered another world where no one would yell at me or throw things. I didn't have to be anyone except who I was. No one judged me. It even seemed like the ladies in the pictures actually wanted to be with me. This started fifteen year captivity. After I became a Christ follower I thought, now I'll finally be free of this. Little did I know that a month later I would be back to my old ways. I would literally yell at God to take it away! This piece of clutter wasn't about to go away easily. It was during this time I met my future wife, Kelly. I was very open and honest with her about my struggle. It wasn't long before we started to talk about marriage. It was at that time I knew I needed to do something drastic. I didn't want to go into our marriage carrying around this life-sucking clutter. Before this I never felt the freedom to talk about my porn clutter with anyone, especially my Christian friends. I absolutely couldn't talk to my pastor about it!

Before I explain what finally broke this chain in my life, I think it's important to understand that the enemy has been using pornography to derail both men and women for a very long time. It has caused calamities in the lives of pastors, politicians, movie stars, sports figures and marriages to name a few. All you have to do is turn on the TV, or look on the internet, and you will see a story where this has cause confusion, chaos and captivity.

There is even a passage of scripture that describes both the lure and toxic outcome of this poisonous clutter. It might not have been called porn, but as we look at some very interesting verses, I guarantee you will see the similarities.

First, you need to understand that the guy who wrote the subsequent verses was the wisest man that ever lived. His name was Solomon. God gave Solomon the ability to observe, navigate and make decisions about life in a way that can only be described as supernatural. One of the books that Solomon wrote is Proverbs, which means "wise sayings". It's in this book that Solomon observes something that was taking place more than 1,000 years before Jesus was born. It all takes place on a street corner while Solomon is watching the events unfold from a window in his house. His window must have been open because he could hear the entire conversation. Solomon could have even been taking notes.

Proverbs 7:6-8 (NLT)
6 While I was at the window of my house, looking through the curtain,
7 I saw some naive young men, and one in particular who lacked common sense.
8 He was crossing the street near the house of an immoral woman, strolling down the path by her house.

Solomon describes the first character in this story as a young man who lacked common sense. How in the world could he have known that by looking out his window? Many scholars believe that this young man knew who lived across the street, like many in his neighborhood. He knew what the women represented, but there was a part of him that was curious. -Sound familiar?

Proverbs 7:9 (NLT)
9 It was at twilight, in the evening, as deep darkness fell.

It wasn't a coincidence that this was about to happen in the dark. What happens in the dark? Secret things. I hate to admit it, but it was in the dark that most of my struggle with porn took place. Darkness doesn't only mean how much light is present, it also means how many people are around. For this young man he waited until it was dark and no one was around to move towards the immoral woman. Sound familiar?

Proverbs 7:10-12 (NLT)
10 The woman approached him, seductively dressed and sly of heart.
11 She was the brash, rebellious type, never content to stay at home.
12 She is often in the streets and markets, soliciting at every corner.

Guys, how many of us would fall for a woman dressed in a snow suit, parka, snow boots and one of those trapper hats. I wonder how many products would lose their appeal with that kind of product girl. The key in verse 10 is: "seductively". She knew exactly what she is doing. Just like a trapper who set's a trap. They make the area around the trap look as good as possible. Even though it looks really good and right, it's hiding something very deadly.

This woman knows the right places to hang out. Porn used to "hang out" exclusively in the streets and market places, now it has a new "street corner" called the internet. Talk about soliciting at every corner! You can get there in just 2 clicks. Sound familiar?

Proverbs 7:13-21 (NLT)
13 She threw her arms around him and kissed him, and with a brazen look she said,
14 "I've just made my peace offerings and fulfilled my vows.
15 You're the one I was looking for! I came out to find you, and here you are!
16 My bed is spread with beautiful blankets, with colored sheets of Egyptian linen.
17 I've perfumed my bed with myrrh, aloes, and cinnamon.
18 Come, let's drink our fill of love until morning. Let's enjoy each other's caresses,
19 for my husband is not home. He's away on a long trip.
20 He has taken a wallet full of money with him and won't return until later this month."
21 So she seduced him with her pretty speech and enticed him with her flattery.

Promises, promises! Solomon wrote down the list of all the things this woman was promising this young man. Let's take a look at his list...

Verse 14 - She is basically saying, look I'm a good person. I'm even a spiritual person who fulfills their vows. You can trust me.

Verse 15 - I've been looking for you all my life! I want to be with you!

Verses 16-17 - You think I look good, you should see where I want to take you! It's better than anything you can imagine.

Verses 18-20 - No one will find out.

Sound familiar?

Solomon, who had heard these promises before, as this woman sank her claws into many a man, also knew what was about to happen next. I can see him thinking to himself, "If you knew what I know, you would be running the other way!" He then writes the sobering truth.

Proverbs 7:22-23 (NLT)
22 He followed her at once, like an ox going to the slaughter. He was like a stag caught in a trap,
23 awaiting the arrow that would pierce its heart. He was like a bird flying into a snare, little knowing it would cost him his life.

Solomon had seen this scenario play itself out numerous times! Always, with the same outcome. If porn is something that is holding you captive, it always, always has the same outcome. Destruction. I saw it played out in my life as well as those whom I've counseled. Solomon even describes the regret attached to this piece of clutter.

Proverbs 5:8-14 (NLT)
8 Stay away from her! Don't go near the door of her house!
9 If you do, you will lose your honor and will lose to merciless people all you have achieved.
10 Strangers will consume your wealth, and someone else will enjoy the fruit of your labor.
11 In the end you will groan in anguish when disease consumes your body.
12 You will say, "How I hated discipline! If only I had not ignored all the warnings!
13 Oh, why didn't I listen to my teachers? Why didn't I pay attention to my instructors?
14 I have come to the brink of utter ruin, and now I must face public disgrace."

Sound familiar?

Let's be honest. If this is something you have struggled with for a long time, it will take more that this chapter to help you break free. I would recommend that you seek out a good Christian counselor that specializes in sexual addictions. Take it from someone who has struggled with this; you can't clean out this clutter on your own.

With that being said, let me share with you what I believe God used to start my victory over porn. It's a 3-step process that will take courage and strength.

Step One
Confess to God

I would suggest you write this out in letter form. As I wrote out my story to God, something took place. First, I was able to better understand how it all began. Second, I was able to be honest about what it was robbing me of. One of the big things was my ability to be intimate with another person. I don't mean in a sexual way, I mean is a transparent, open and honest way. Third, it reminded me how much God loved me, because I didn't feel God's anger, I felt His love, compassion and desire to help me break free! I had repented thousands of times, but after I wrote it out, God's Spirit brought to my mind a verse.

Romans 5:8 (NLT)
8 But God showed his great love for us by sending Christ to die for us while we were still sinners.

No condemnation! Just grace!

Step Two
Confess to others

Remember in our story how it took place in the dark? Anytime you keep something in the dark it will have control over you. It's not until you bring it into the light that you begin to experience freedom. For me, freedom didn't begin until I was willing to share my porn addiction with someone I trusted. It took me years before I had the courage to share this face-to-face. It happened while I was on a summer project with "Campus Crusade for Christ". A good friend that came into my life that summer seemed like a safe person with whom I could share my deep dark secret. I will never forget our conversation. We met at a little sandwich coffee shop place. In the middle of my roast turkey and alfalfa sprout sandwich, I decided to spill the beans. I felt like I could puke at any moment. Then the words came out. I don't know how they sounded. To me they sounded all garbled. After I was done telling him the whole story. I just sat there waiting for some kind of nice rebuke. Instead, he looked at me and said, "Brother, sounds to me like this stuff is kicking your butt." I said, "You have no idea." Then he said something I didn't expect. "Yes I do." Porn had a hold on my life for almost 10 years. I sat there silent for what seemed an eternity. This guy, who I had put on a huge pedestal, just told me he had experienced the same struggle!

Over the next months he was able to help me come to grips with my addiction. I read as much as I could. There wasn't a whole lot out there about porn addictions at that time. But when I brought it out into the light I felt like a huge weight was taken off.

Did you know that God promises us healing when we tell someone else about our sin?

James 5:16 (NLT)
16 Confess your sins to each other and pray for each other so that you may be healed. The earnest prayer of a righteous person has great power and produces wonderful results.

Step Three
Be Accountable

The raw truth about this kind of clutter is that you will need help from others to help you clean it out and keep it from coming back. Back in the 80's and early 90's there wasn't much out there to help facilitate accountability in this area except weekly meetings with an accountability partner. Even having accountability partners isn't always the answer, especially if they struggle too and your times together center around how you've only looked at porn twice versus six times that week. I'm not saying that having a group of men to hold you accountable isn't a good idea. Make sure they are the kind of men who are safe and victorious in this area. I wanted to be around men who have actually cleaned it ALL out of their lives and have a track record of keeping it out. You have to be willing to ask each other the hard questions and be honest.

With the internet, the battle has ramped up dramatically! I have had enough conversations with men to know it's the number one place we go. Fortunately there is accountability software out there that can help keep you accountable with individuals you trust. There's even a website the specializes in helping Christ followers recognize this clutter and provide you with a game plan to clean it out of your life. It's called triplexchurch.com. It's one of the few websites on the web that deals directly with pornography and Christians. They have both a free version and a pro version of software, "xwatch" that will track your website browsing and send email printouts of all questionable sites to specific individuals every two weeks. When you know they will be getting that printout, it makes you think twice! They have recently added a 30 day online workshop designed to help you break free of porn. I've used it in our men's group with great success.

Final Thoughts

For those of you who are married, let me give you some final thoughts on this. I told my wife about my struggle before we even got married. I didn't want any skeletons in my closet to poke their ugly head out after we started out life together. If this is something you are trying to hide from you wife, let me give you a piece of advice: don't. It will surface somehow, some way. Porn actually robs you of the ability to be intimate with your wife. She will notice. The consequences of concealment are a lot worse than the consequences of confession. Tell her of your struggle, ask her for forgiveness and seek help.

Chapter 8

Keep Going!

As I was thinking about how I wanted to finish this book, one final question came to my mind. It's a question that I have asked numerous times in my attempt to clean out the clutter in my life. For you, it's a question that if you haven't asked it already, you should.

How do I keep going?

Once I think I'm making progress in cleaning out one piece of clutter, another one rears its ugly head. How in the world do we keep moving forward when everything is screaming at us to stop? The key is found in the rest of the verses we started with at the very beginning of this book.

Hebrews 12:1-3 (NLT)
1 Therefore, since we are surrounded by such a huge crowd of witnesses to the life of faith, let us strip off every weight that slows us down, especially the

**sin that so easily trips us up. And let us run with
endurance the race God has set before us.**

Remember those two kinds of clutter?
A. Weight that slows us down
B. Sin that trips us up

According to this verse, if we strip this clutter off we
will be able to run with endurance. I used to run a lot.
I can't anymore because my knees rebel. The longest I
have ever run is about 19 miles. Anyone who runs a lot
will tell you there are "walls" you hit during a long run.
Everything inside of you is screaming for you to stop!
The key is to keep your pace and NOT STOP. I used to
get these cramps that my coach would call "stitches".
Every time I would get them, he would tell me to just
keep going and they would go away. He was right.
Eventually that feeling of wanting to stop fades and
somehow you're able to push past the "wall" and keep
going. There were even times when I felt energized and
ready to go farther than I thought I ever could!

In my own life I have hit many "walls". Sometimes
I've actually stopped. Like in a long run, if you stop it's
really hard to start running again. But, the times when
I didn't stop and I kept going, I was able to push on and
reach towards my goal. It wasn't will power that helped
me keep going. It wasn't the fact that I'm some kind
of super spiritual maverick. Anybody that knows me
will tell you that I'm not. The only times I have been
able to keep going is when I've been able to remember

a simple, yet powerful truth. It all centers around the next 2 verses of Hebrews 12:

2 We do this by keeping our eyes on Jesus, the champion who initiates and perfects our faith. Because of the joy awaiting him, he endured the cross, disregarding its shame. Now he is seated in the place of honor beside God's throne.
3 Think of all the hostility he endured from sinful people; then you won't become weary and give up.

These are some very powerful truths, that if embraced, will help you not only start the clutter cleaning process, but give you the endurance to finish the job. Somehow there is a way to not grow weary and give up, even though every cell in your body is screaming to stop. Let's unpack these truths one a time.

Keep Your Eyes Focused On Jesus!
I used to live in Nebraska and North Dakota. There was lots of land, and lots of farms, and I had lots of friends with both. I will never forget the day I spent with a friend who was plowing his field. Don't ask me how many acres he had. All I know is we were in that tractor for hours. I was amazed at how straight his rows were. And as we drove and talked, he never looked back. He always looked straight ahead. I couldn't figure out how he did it! Finally after about an hour I asked him how in the world his rows were so straight even though he never looked behind him. Then he said something that didn't make sense until years later. He said, "if you

want to finish with nice straight rows you can't look behind. When you start looking behind the tractor's going to go where it wants to go. When I focus on a point in front of me I know the tractor will follow straight and true".

It's so easy to focus on our past failures, our past mistakes and our past attempts at cleaning out our clutter. When I've done that, I have veered all over the place! It wasn't until I focused on who this is really about, that I was able to get back on track. Like that fixed point my farmer friend had, Jesus is our fixed point that will help us keep moving forward straight and true."

Why Jesus? He's Been There!

If you've ever gone through a really gut wrenching experience it always helps to talk to someone who's gone through the same thing and come out on the other side. Especially if they point to specific things that kept them going. The next question you should be asking yourself is "why Jesus?" How can focusing on who Jesus is help? Well, I could give you the typical church answer, "He's God's Son, and you can trust Him". Which is true, but if you're neck deep in your clutter you might want something a little more tangible. Fortunately, in his letter to the Hebrews, Paul didn't use that answer. He took it to a personal level. He reminded the Hebrews, and now us that Jesus has been there. He had a race to finish just like we do. In fact,

He's the perfect example for us to follow. Jesus created the model of what it would take to live the Christian life. It's a model based on His own experience during His life as a human being. In fact the word used for "initiates" has to do with a pioneer. Someone who blazes the trail for all those that follow. Jesus wasn't cleaning out His own clutter, but was confronted by the toxic clutter of others. Even Jesus wanted to stop, but He kept going. I love how the message expresses this verse:

Hebrews 12:2-3 (MSG)
2 Keep your eyes on Jesus, who both began and finished this race we're in. Study how he did it. Because he never lost sight of where he was headed—that exhilarating finish in and with God— he could put up with anything along the way: cross, shame, whatever. And now he's there, in the place of honor, right alongside God.
3 When you find yourselves flagging in your faith, go over that story again, item by item, that long litany of hostility he plowed through. That will shoot adrenaline into your souls!

In these few choice verses, Jesus gives us what I call the endurance model for living the Christian life and finishing the race. Our Christian life isn't a 100 yard dash or a marathon. It's a steeple chase! Lots of things to fall into and climb over.

Just so you know that Jesus really does understand our clutter take a look some of what He experienced:

Even before He was born an **angry** person tried to murder him - Matthew 2:16

Because of **fear** one of His closest friends denied Him. - Luke 22:54-61

Because of the **lust** for power and money He was betrayed - Luke 22:47

Because of **his past**, Peter didn't feel worthy of God's grace - Luke 5:8

Because of **unforgiveness** a brother wasn't willing to except a father's love for his son - Luke 15:25-30

Jesus talked about the reality of **worry** - Matthew 6:19-34

Jesus was born into a clutter filled world! He knew what He was in for. He knew what it was going to take to endure and finish the race.

If we don't know how to endure the ups and downs, we are sunk. In the process of cleaning out your clutter I guarantee you will need endurance! According to Jesus, the endurance model for living the Christian life has everything to do with your focus. Even the creator of the Universe, who became a human being needed something to focus on if He was to finish His race. It wasn't His abilities, His failures or His past. Jesus focused on the number one thing that kept Him going and will keep you and I going...

Jesus focused on His promised future with God at the end of the race.

Jesus knew that this human experience was brief. It wasn't all there was. There would be a time when all the striving, planning and struggles would be over. Although the way was tough and at times seemed unbearable, Jesus knew if He focused on God's promise of a future with Him, He could endure anything! I sometimes forget that Jesus has been around forever. He had already experienced some of eternity before coming to earth. He knows just how short our lives are as human beings.

When I speak on this subject I bring with me a 500 foot long yellow rope on a huge spool. Since I'm a very visual person it helps me to visualize just how short my life is. I choose people at different places around the sanctuary. I walk around with the rope having my volunteers hold on to it as I pass them. Eventually the entire sanctuary is encircled by this yellow rope. Then walk out through one of the doors telling everyone that it's going on for eternity. I walk back on stage and relieve the volunteer holding the beginning of the rope. I've colored about 2 inches of it red. I then tell the audience that the yellow part of the rope represents eternity and the red part represents our life.

The reality is that the color of the rope we focus on determines how we live our life. For a lot of Christ followers, because their focus is on this life, they never experience the freedom, the joys and the God-realities that propel them forward. The reason why we choose not to clean out the clutter is if it's all about this life, then it's not worth the struggle. But, the reality is it's not about this short life that scripture calls a vapor. It's about an eternity that is waiting for us with God. It's about a place that Jesus has been getting ready for us for a very long time!

John 14:1-3 (NLT)
1 "Don't let your hearts be troubled. Trust in God, and trust also in me.
2 There is more than enough room in my Father's home. If this were not so, would I have told you that I am going to prepare a place for you?
3 When everything is ready, I will come and get you, so that you will always be with me where I am.

Jesus wanted to make it very clear that this life is not all there is. This is not our home. We were not created as permanent residents! God never intended us to stay here forever. He did intend for us to look forward to what we would experience once we we're done here. He knows we need something to look forward to so we don't grow weary and give up. If you've ever looked forward to a vacation you have experienced just a little how this works. Let's say you're leaving by the end of the week on a much deserved, all-expense paid, vacation.

All of a sudden the things that normally bother you aren't that big of a deal. Yeah, you're probably pulling your hair out, if you have any, trying to get everything done, but for some reason you can do it because you know at the end of the week no matter what happens, you're gone! That focus on just "getting it done so you can go" is what I believe Paul is trying to explain to us. Jesus came here to get it done! He knew all the clutter He would have to endure in order to finish His race. One of the things that kept Him going was the reality of what was waiting for him at the finish line.

So what are some of the promises we can focus on? I'm glad you asked!
Here are just a few......

Promises for strength and endurance
When I feel like I can't go on, God's grace kicks in! 2 Corinthians 12:9-10

Getting rid of clutter is a struggle that others have faced and conquered. Romans 7:14-25

God has unlimited resources He wants to empower you with! Ephesians 3:14-16

When I stop relying on my own efforts and turn to God, He will supply what I need! 2 Corinthians 1:8-10

God has power we can ask for to help us endure! Colossians 1:11

Our endurance can actually grow! James 1:2-4

God can replace weakness with strength! Isaiah 40:29-31

Promises for a future with God

We will get new bodies! Romans 8:23, 2 Corinthians 5:1-10

There is a place that is being prepared just for us! John 14:1-3

If I have placed my faith in Jesus, He will take me home! I Thessalonians 4:13-18

Heaven is a real place! Revelation 21:15-27

Nothing can separate me from God's love! Romans 8:31-39

We can trust God's promises! I Timothy 1:12

Jesus promises to bring us home! John 14:3

Jesus actually wants to be with me! John 17:24

I will be with Jesus forever! I Thessalonians 4:17

Our home will be with God and He will be with us! Revelation 21:3

Final Thoughts

I hope as you read this you realized that cleaning out your clutter isn't rocket science. It's a simple one-step-at a-time process. Some of the clutter will take longer to clean than you thought, while other clutter can be swept up in just a few moments. The hardest part of all this is admitting what kind of clutter you have, then begin the process of cleaning it out.

Let me leave you with a passage of scripture that has become a great encouragement to me. As someone who is still in the process of cleaning out his clutter, it's good to know that God is committed to helping me finish the job!

Philippians 1:6 (NLT)
6 And I am certain that God, who began the good work within you, will continue his work until it is finally finished on the day when Christ Jesus returns.

Philippians 1:6 (MSG)
6 There has never been the slightest doubt in my mind that the God who started this great work in you would keep at it and bring it to a flourishing finish on the very day Christ Jesus appears.

Philippians 1:6 (NASB77)
6 For I am confident of this very thing, that He who began a good work in you will perfect it until the day of Christ Jesus.

If you would like more information about the ministry of That Neighborhood Church check out our website at www.lovegodlovepeopleproveit.com

Made in the USA
Lexington, KY
04 September 2014